MW00615330

TO: DEE

CHRISTOPHER.
XXX.

First Edition: 2008.

Unedited versions of portions of this book were published online on Christopher Gutierrez' online journal, askheychris.livejournal.com.

ISBN-10: 0-9777665-3-5

ISBN-13: 978-0-9777665-3-6

Printed in the United States.
Published by The Deadxstop Publishing Company.

Cover design by Jean-Paul Frijns
jeanpaul@valueofstrength.com
Interior page layout by Daniel Polyak
Edited by Laura Prusik

Deadxstop.com
Askheychris.livejournal.com
Myspace.com/thedeadxstoppublishingcompany

Christopher Gutierrez

notes from the deep end

a year in the life of a touring author

the deadxstop publishing company
Chicago

For Heather Ferrari.
Who made this possible.

"You tell me that I make no difference, at least I'm fucking trying.
What the fuck have you done?"

- *In my eyes*, Minor Threat

Introduction
❖

I have always been a bit of a coward. Unsure and awkward, even my first memory is one of gutlessness.

I was almost three years old, riding my red tricycle down the sidewalk when an older neighborhood kid walked up on my right side, grabbed my handlebars and tried to pull the tricycle out from under me. I wouldn't let go, so he shoved me off and onto the ground. I laid there and cried, well because, that's what you do when you're a little kid. But the thing that hovers over that memory is the fact that I could have held on harder. I could have hit back. I knew how to hit at that age. My first memory is of being a wimp.

As time progressed and I watched my friends go off to college and get degrees or turn humble basement bands into successful radio juggernauts, I sat back and watched. Sure, I had my adventures along the way, but I never really gave anything my all.

I have never stayed up all night studying for a test.

I have never chased after a girlfriend following a fight.

I have never dropped everything to help anyone in my family.

I have never drove through the night to stand outside of a woman's window to scream out my undying love.

It is a constant theme in every aspect of my love and life. I lack passion and I know it. But how does one attain passion? I mean, isn't that something you're born with? You shouldn't have to search for passion within yourself. It should ooze out of your pores and imbed itself into every kiss, every sentence and every song.

We are all born with a passion; it's just sabotaged by reluctance, apprehension and intimidation. Passionate motherfuckers refuse to be held back by convention. By comfort. By approval. By disapproval. By lack of time, money or sleep. They go. They get into it. They get it on. They don't look back because they're too busy thrashing forward. And I have sat back for years watching. Watching. Watching the same buildings, trains, sidewalks, venues and television sets.

This book is not about watching.

This is a book filled with promises about the only passion I know.

It is my fight. My life. My light.

It is my testimony of chins up, fingers crossed and eyes wide open.

Because while my first memory may be of one of being a wimp...

I promise you, my last will not be.

Monday, June 25, 2007
3:30 a.m. Newark, Delaware
❖

I walked in early, but the room was already packed. South Street in Philadelphia.

The kids.

The kids; some laugh, some stare, some take pictures and some shake nervously when I hug them. They're so innocent. I was that kid. I was them. I still am them.

They tell me that I am their hero. How should I respond to that? Seriously, how?

"You're my hero. I really look up to you."

Somehow my simple response of "thank you" just seems to deflate the power in their words. I know this, and the kids know this. I wish my words didn't diminish the immensity of their words.

I look to the floor and wish that they wouldn't have said it, only because my heart and head do not have the capacity to wrap themselves around those words. I know how difficult it is to allow yourself to be so vulnerable. It's like I want to grab each one of these kids by the shoulders and say, "Listen you, save these words for someone real, someone who can take those words and turn them into band-aids for your scars, not some sham with a god complex and racing stripes."

But I don't. Because at 4 a.m. in dank and moist hotel rooms in tiny states, I realize that, as trite and self-absorbed as it may sound, maybe I *AM* all they have. Maybe I am their hero. So now what? What should I do with this?

When sports players would exit the courthouse of whatever

13

shooting, rape or gambling trial they were attending, I always heard the same thing come out of their mouths, "I didn't ask to be a role model."

And it made sense. Just because they can dribble a ball faster, swing a bat with more precision or run defensive maneuvers better than 99 percent of the population doesn't mean that they should be looked to as the moral standard for our society. I get that. But what they didn't get, in all of their million dollar deals and television commercials, is that whether they asked for it or not they have responsibility thrust upon them. That label. Those expectations. These kids with no one else to turn to held out their faith and trust and attached it to the backs of these people (and mine) because they have found something in us. What that is, I'll never see, but they do. And maybe, just maybe those kids see more clearly than we who look in mirrors and see surface and smog. Maybe it's those kids who signed up for the thankless job of holding up our hearts, because they believed in us all along because they knew we, ourselves, couldn't. Because hearts actively seek out other hearts that need love the most, whether they deserve it or not, and in most cases, not.

Just because I don't believe it doesn't make it untrue. Because truth is subjective, and those words and their faith are real, even if the shine is smudged from my view. And while I didn't ask for it, it's there, sitting on my back. And while I might not be able to see it, I keep turning around and around like a dog chasing its tail so that one day, hopefully, I'll be able to catch a glimpse of what they see. I owe them at least to keep chasing.

The progress I am making in these last days of my first real book tour is astounding. The kids walk in and think that I am there to entertain them. But what they don't know is that the entertainment is the simple by product of my grand scheme: to vomit the horrors of my life out of my head and into the eyes and the ears of kids across America. They are the custodial engineers of my emotional smog factory. I breathe out the poison, and the kids, with their wide-eyes and open hearts, filter the carcinogens from my blood.

I owe them. Because they make this machine move forward.

And I love them.

Or maybe the idea of them.

But what's so wrong with that?

Tuesday, June 26, 2007
2:25 a.m. Philadelphia, Pennsylvania
❖

Somehow I always manage to find my way back here. Lying in a bunk in a bus full of friends. The bus has 12 compartments, six on each side and 10 people on the bus. As with most bands on buses, one bunk is used as an extra storage compartment and universally referred to as a "junk bunk." Luckily, their bass tech ditched out for some reason and that freed up an empty space for my ass. Since I need to be in Brooklyn tomorrow for the last date on my book tour, I managed to snake a free ride with my friends in the band, Rise Against.

Since last night I was in the Philadelphia area, and I knew my friends would be in town the next day, I decided to stay an extra day to spend some time with them. They tour about 10 months out of the year and are rarely home in Chicago.

The singer, Tim, is one of the most sincere people I have ever had the pleasure of calling my friend. I've known him for years, ever since I replaced him as the bass player in the old Chicago hardcore band, Arma Angelus. He is one of those people who is not only talented, intelligent and fortunate but possesses the uncanny ability to handle every aspect of his life with style, grace and humility, which is not only rare but damn near extinct in this business. I truly look up to him as a model of character and compassion. He is so driven, yet will spend as much time as you will allow talking about his wife and his daughter. Tim used to stop by and I would cut his hair while he sat straddling the toilet in my bathroom. Now I'm not a fan of children, but after his daughter Blythe was born, Tim would bring her by my apartment. She was the first baby I held in my arms that didn't feel like a time bomb.

I've known Joe who plays bass since I roadied for his old band, 88 Fingers Louie more than a decade ago.

It's a marvelous feeling to watch your friends play with such passion and drive that you notice that you have goosebumps. Something about the line, "Now there's a reason, to give it all" hit me tonight like a cinderblock to the chest. He makes me feel that there are other people in this world who see the same magic I do.

I never sleep well the in bunks. The engine is loud, people snore and while moving I feel like I'm being rocked back and forth in the hull of the Mayflower. Oh, and every morning when I wake up and attempt to sit up, I smash my forehead into the low ceiling.

The bus is moving and I'm sloshing around already. I have shoved in my earplugs, and I am prepared to do battle with the darkness of this coffin.

Wednesday, June 27, 2007
1:50 a.m. West New York, New Jersey
❖

The tour ended tonight in Brooklyn in a sweat-filled rant about living deliberate. I felt the tears squeeze their way into the corners of my eyes and I did my best to hold them back, not because I was afraid of expressing myself but because I didn't want the words that were coming out of my mouth and heart to be overshadowed by the fact that "Chris lost it on stage."

I wanted everyone to understand how much their attention and support of my little dream meant to me, but I don't think I communicated it as well as I could have. When I hug the kids, I try to make them feel that I will do my best to live up to their trust. I try to do that with a hug. I just hope someone feels it.

Afterward, a group of friends and I took a train to get food. We sat around and talked music because that's what we all have in common. What bands do wrong, what they do right and what we would do in their position. Apparently, if my friends and I started a management company, we would be churning out Led Zeppelin and Green Day careers like diarrhea after a late night dinner of bad Mexican food.

Currently I am staying directly across the Hudson River in New Jersey with my friends Mikey and Alicia, sitting on their couch, each on our own laptop. Both good people I met in my travels on tours over the years.

Alicia dated a friend of mine a few years ago. When I met her I was immediately floored. Not only was she ridiculously attractive, but she shared my love for The History Channel and bad metal music, as well.

Mikey, I met around the same time while his band My Chemical Romance was on the Vans Warped Tour and we were introduced through a mutual friend. I was told, "Dude, Mikey is so rad. He'll hang out with anyone. He doesn't care if you're famous or in a band." Mikey was sitting next to me. I wasn't sure if that was a compliment or an insult, either way, we get along like peas and carrots because he shares my obsession for transformer toys. When we hang out, it feels like a 6th grade sleepover because we just stay up late gossiping, watching movies and eating crappy food.

I wish I lived closer to them.

Thursday, June 28, 2007
3:30 a.m. Philadelphia, Pennsylvania
❖

God truly does have a sense of humor. See, god knows when I want something so badly that he will take pains to watch me squirm as he dashes my hopes of sleeping in a warm bed. It's not that I don't want to be on tour anymore, but you know when you have begun to mentally prepare for something to be over with? Like when you're in the movie and you think the massive Hobbit battle was a perfect and epic ending of a trilogy but then you have to wade through an extra 30 minutes of homo-erotic Shire touchy-feely man/boy love, you know that disappointment that seems to overshadow all of that ass-kicking tree madness. Yes, oh my faithfuls, that is the disappointment that I feel now.

I have been rolling through the country, standing on stages and pushing with all of my might the words that have spent 32 years affecting the direction of my love and growth. But now, I have stormed those walls and taken my horrors by the neck to hold them up to crowd and say, "Look at what I caught!" Like a proud and grinning little kid with his first fishing conquest.

The sweat dripped from my chin even before I stepped on that stage last night. I walked in and felt the hair on my head begin to curl at the base and my upper lip shimmer with liquid. I arrived late at the coffee shop in Brooklyn because the Q train was running hot and slow. But I made it. And kids and adults showed up. Many for the third and fourth times, which is still a little overwhelming for me because I can see in their faces that they believe in my dream just as much as I do, and I feel like I owe them all of the honesty I know how to give. It was difficult to get into my groove last night because of the heat and the pressure to give the kids fresh and new stories. It's more difficult than I thought it would be. I see how bands and speakers fall into a rut of doing the same performance over and over again. Like when you go see that band you love, and they tell that funny joke and you think it's just for you. That is, until you go to see them a few days later in a different town and hear the same funny joke at the same time in the same set. I don't want to be that band or that guy. I don't want it to end, and I usually try to get off the stage before people start looking at their watches because I was told by a former band-mate years ago that when entertaining, you should always leave your audience wanting more. But I couldn't set that microphone down. I wanted every soul in that room to understand that I was trying my damnedest to love them. To make them understand how grateful I was and to not squander the moment that floated in the air.

Today, Mikey and Alicia took me to Chinatown to buy knockoff luggage. It was so hot that our jeans looked elastic and our hair curled at the ends. Afterward, I took a shuttle to the airport to find that since it rained in the Midwest, flights were canceled. I stood in a line for 3.5 hours to have some over-worked airline representative tell me in her thickest Jersey accent, "I got nuthin for you 'til late Friday night, honey."

I wanted to yell at her, "But ... but, I really need to sleep in my own bed tonight. No really, I'm mentally prepared for it and everything!"

After hours of talking with my agent and friend Heather, she found that if I could get to Philadelphia, I could catch a flight to Columbus, Ohio, where a friend from the internet could pick me up and drop me off in Indianapolis, where my girlfriend Lindsie could pick me up and take me back to my soft, warm bed and not give me fellatio. So I hopped in a limo. Now don't get the impression that I roll like that, but the cabs were out to rob everyone tonight and were charging $140 for a trip to Newark. The limos, on the other hand, were only charging $68. I get to Newark, shit, get a coffee with so much sugar my straw literally did stand up straight, then met up with some wonderful and generous internet friends who drove me the hour and a half to drop me off here in Philadelphia. Another night with no sleep. It's strange ... the older I get, the less sleep I need.

Friday, June 29, 2007
5:51 p.m. Chicago, Illinois
❖

Apparently I made it home fine, or at least the futuristic version of me found my secret journals and has mastered the fine art of butchering the English language with a total disregard for sentence structure, just like the real flesh-and-blood, greasy-faced version of me.

Last time we spoke I was lying up against the curbside baggage check window waiting for the handlers to show. They did so I flew out to Columbus where a friend of mine, Justin picked me up. I managed to get two hours of sleep at the baggage claim underneath the payphones. I figured if I put my luggage under the phones it would be in plain view of everyone, thereby discouraging the hoodlums from stealing them out in the open. It's incredible how quickly I can force myself to sleep when I'm in public, yet I have trouble lying in my own bed at home.

Justin drove me the 3.5 hours from Columbus to Indianapolis so I could meet up with my girlfriend, the ferret.

So Chris, why is it that you refer to her as the ferret?

Have you ever picked up a ferret? Have you ever tried to just chill and cuddle with a ferret on the couch? What happened when you let the ferret walk around your apartment? Have you ever tried to love a ferret?

Do you remember those rubber water snake toys you could buy from the grocery store toy section when you were a kid? The fun is in trying to hold it in your hand but the tighter you squeeze, the more it slips away. You know, they kind of resemble a flaccid and uncircumcised penis? That's what ferrets are, the animal version of that. And my girlfriend is the living and breathing and stripping version of a ferret. Trying to love her is maybe the most challenging thing I've ever done. She is a lit firecracker in my palm. I laugh and smile and get the biggest rush, all while testing to see how much adrenaline my senses can handle. Yeah. It feels that good. Somehow I have a feeling I'm going to end up with scorch marks across my face but goddamn it all to hell, it's adventure like I've never felt before from a woman and fuck if it doesn't amazing to feel the blood pump through my veins. She is my pusher.

After I arrived in Indianapolis, she drove me home.

Home is different now. Home is a re-charge station, a docking station. It's glue.

Saturday, June 30, 2007
10 p.m. Chicago, Illinois
❖

Today I met up with a person I don't really know very well. How or why I met her is irrelevant because she could be anyone. She sat across from me and told me that people make her feel less than she is. I asked her why she lets them make her feel that way, and she looked at me like I was speaking Japanese.

"How do I *let* them make me feel that way?" she asked.

I told her how after the sting of the first five seconds, she, her, I, all of us determine how we let words affect us. She said that I was stronger than she was. I chuckled, sat up, put my hands on the table and said, "You have two hands and two legs and a heart and a brain and the ability to reason just like I do. It's just somewhere along the line, someone told you that you weren't good enough and you were silly enough to believe them."

I could see that she was letting down her guard. She told me that she had been hurt. I told her we all have. She told me how so many people have betrayed her. I looked away and said, "But somehow, despite everything, you're still here talking, laughing, loving. Those people obviously didn't do a good job at breaking your heart, or else we wouldn't be here talking. You would be dead."

We talked and she cried, and we hung out and bullshitted. I hugged her and told her I was leaving. She asked me not to and I asked why, and she said, "Because when you leave I will be alone. I hate being by myself." I stayed a little longer and as I stood to leave, I asked if she would be ok. She said yes. I asked if she was done for being sensitive artist for the evening and she blew up on me. She yelled, "I am not a fucking joke." I tried to explain to her that I meant no harm and that it was just my shitty expression. She kept yelling about things she thought I said, or things she thought I meant. Then it dawned upon me, she was upset that I was leaving. Abandoning her when she was at her most vulnerable, just like everyone else in her life had done to her. I tried to reason with her and make her understand that she was just projecting her insecurities and feelings of rejection upon me and that I wasn't the one that should be the target, especially after talking with her at length about her problems. Apparently she wouldn't like it when I pointed out how "right" I was. Who knew?

I left feeling terrible. I could hear her sobbing as I walked away. I wanted to walk back and hug her but I didn't. Because I can't save people. People save themselves. She wasn't my mess to clean up. But I tried, I swear I did. I tried to reason with her and give her examples of what I believe to be true. I tried to explain to her my never-fail coping mechanisms. I tried, but in the end I realized that some people are far too damaged, and my lack of training and my dime-store field kit can't perform open-heart surgery.

I may pack up my tools and move on, but I will keep trying. Because somewhere along the line, I will patch up some holes. The odds are in my favor.

Monday, July 2, 2007
10:39 p.m. Somewhere Over the
Atlantic Ocean
❖

I've come to the recent discovery that the key to maintaining healthy relationships is appreciation. We all simply want to feel appreciated. So if I have the key to this, why is it that I manage to sabotage so many relationships? Friends, family, women; if I know this, why am I so reluctant to make them feel appreciated? And again, simple answer: because I want them to fail.

Another truth I've come to realize is that most relationships are out of convenience. Wow, what a revelation, Chris, right? Yeah, I know, nothing any little pocket-sized self-help book couldn't tell me. But what's even more important than this moment of clarity is, why? I mean, how do we get there?

Historically, most relationships I've known have progressed something like this; boy meets girl. Boy (or girl) is enamored and pursues because one or many attributes are attractive. Girl either finds similar or comparable attributes attractive in the pursuer and they get together. "Get together" is a loose and subjective term. At some point, the relationship becomes exclusive for one of many reasons ... but in most cases, in the end when everyone has the balls to be completely honest with themselves, the issue of exclusivity is simply because one does not want the other person to "kiss" other people. Follow me...

Boy likes girl.
Girl likes boy.

They kiss.
They kiss again.
Boy would like to kiss other girls.
Girl notes that boys like to kiss girls.
Girl suggests commitment.
Boy is boyfriend, girl is girlfriend.
"Committed relationship."
Of course, this is a sweeping generalization. Admittedly, a handful of couples do get together because of that "I'll never love another-take my heart and bury it inside your chest-I'll walk through snowstorms to save your life" type of love. But come on, most don't. I can say this confidently because hey, how many of *your* relationships failed. Is the answer "most"?
Convenience.
Fine, I'll admit it. And if convenience wasn't the motivation at the start, it certainly was the motivation to maintain. I simply perpetuated a relationship, whether consciously or subconsciously, that I knew was doomed. And sometimes I made that realization in the first few weeks and sometimes it took until a few years afterward.

Either way, I just don't want my chick to make out with other dudes. I'll admit it. And yes, that has been the primary motivation behind most of my relationships. I would hate to think that any current and future relationships would end with similar results but fuck; I don't really have much of a track record.

She was unbelievably attractive. She sat in my chair while I highlighted her hair and I fumbled words. We talked. We texted. She came over. We kissed. We fucked. She came over again the next day. We talked. We kissed. We fucked. She wasn't the brightest but she had a light and a life about her ... and um, yeah and she was unbelievably attractive. She was fun, even if she couldn't relate. We laid in bed and she listened to me talk at her. I spoke of my dreams and aspirations because at 3 a.m. on dark and cold nights when it's just you and her lying next to each other, nothing makes a boy more dreamy. I know this. But luckily, that's just what comes out of my mouth at that time with a female in my bed. After a few weeks, she was my girlfriend because she knew I wanted to make out with other girls, and she simply didn't want me to. We kissed and she told me she loved me. I smiled, kissed her on her forehead and said thank you. We dated for a few months until she laid her cards out on the table for me. She showed me what she was playing with in hopes that I would take a shot. A chance on her.

I didn't take the bet.

In the end, I realized that the only reason I agreed to be in that committed relationship was because I didn't want her to make out with other dudes, as well. I didn't feel good about it, but it called into question my motivation behind my previous relationships. They were "good enough." And looking back, I knew that.

Now, typing these words on a bumpy flight to Amsterdam, I can see it was because that's what I have always felt I've deserved. Because that's what I am.

"Good enough."

I've always joked with people, "Hey, you know me, I'm always a B+."

It's a B+ life.

Like the village leper, I never really understand what it is that people see. I get it; I'm a good fisherman. I can say all the right words and glance at you out of the corner of my eye for those few seconds and brush the hairs out of your face in just the right way to implant my master plan into your head. I'm a good fisherman. But at some point, the fisherman just wants to go home to jerk off, take a dump and watch TV, and that's where I fade.

But really, I just want someone to look at me and say, "Thank you for letting me love you, Chris," and mean it. As arrogant and selfish as it may sound, I need to know that that is the kind of love I'm dealing with, because then, then I will walk through snowstorms to save your life.

Wednesday, July 4, 2007
8:40 p.m. Somewhere in the Belgium Countryside
❖

What I don't and can't seem to grasp about the human condition is the reluctance to rage. Well, maybe rage is the wrong word here. Maybe it is people's fear of passion, or their fear of allowing the passion within them the opportunity to run around the world tearing up the carpet and pissing on things.

I understand fear. I do. I am a self-professed recovering pussy. I was the kid who was always a little too small and too girly for his age ... and honestly, I still am. The product of bad genes and being raised by women. Until recently, it has been something that I have always felt ashamed of. I was taught to be in touch with my senses, to love things hard, to purge my insecurities, to hold on to the things I hold dear and to try new salad dressings. I cried the night I talked that girl into being my first girlfriend. I clutched my little paws on my chest

27

and breathed in and out deeply through my mouth because my sinuses were draining down my face along with tears of happiness. Of course I never told a soul. And right now, while one of my best friends in the world, Nyree, sleeps quietly in the seat directly across from me and this train speeds its way though the countryside of Belgium toward the most romantic city in the world, I'm looking over my right shoulder and staring at the colors of a rainbow. My heart is full. No ... bursting at the reds and yellows and blues and greens that cross the cloudy sky above the pastures while the black and white cows graze. And I will never tell a soul.

Except you.

I want to call my friends and tell them that they make me proud, that I have wonderful people who believe in me and my intentions in life and that one day I want to love them with the passion with which they deserve. I want to call my mother and tell her she is my one and only true hero. That I wish she could be in this seat next to me, holding my hand while silently staring out the window at the wet buildings that have lined these railroad tracks for a hundred years. I wish I could dig my fingers deep into the exterior of this machine and dig out the guts and lifeblood that provide the steam and momentum for this engine and give that energy to those that hold my heart. But the only way I can make that happen is to live in a manner that I believe is making the most of my potential. Because I see their eyes when they hug me and like overhearing a parent brag about their children, I hear their voices twinge with pride when they speak of me to others because it's not what they are saying, it's how they are saying it.

See, it just makes sense, to want to see, hear, taste, smell and touch everything this world has to offer. I want to feel the sands of Africa in my teeth and kiss black women on the mouth. I want to stare at animals and collide with friends who are dancing along to the same beat that moves my feet and their fists. I want to grit my teeth during sex then hold her so close that I crave to be inside her skin. I want to throw myself into the shark-infested waters to see if I can make it back alive. And while I may forget this quiet ride from Amsterdam to Paris one day, I damn sure won't forget the way it made me feel.

Because to live contently and comfortablely in front of a television set, to work docile and mundane careers for other people's dreams will be the death of me. And I owe my friends, my mother, the people that I tell of my world, and I owe the sands of Africa I have yet to taste.

So that one day, when this engine is so beaten and battered that I barely recognize it, hopefully I can look down and trace these battle scars and racing stripes and be able to see what others see in me.

No, maybe passion is the wrong word, maybe the word IS rage.

Thursday, July 5, 2007
11:55 p.m. On a train leaving Paris
❖

I won't lie, the first time I was in France I was a bit disappointed that it wasn't exactly like the France I remember from the movie "Bon Voyage Charlie Brown." I wanted so badly to see the seedy looking pubs illuminated with a single candle, instead I got fake ass gangbanger kids who sounded like chef from the Muppet movies.

It's funny how the worlds we create in our minds get crushed by the weight of reality. It is the killer of romanticism. But time and distance will usually make up for that loss.

Every time I am in Europe, I exclusively listen to Euro bands. I don't know, it just feels like I'm immersing myself into their culture just that much more. I know, totally ridiculous, right? Today, as I lay in a bunk in an over-night train from Paris to Irun, Spain, I'm listening to Karl Larrson. The solo record from the singer of one of my favorite bands of all time, The Last Days of April, who I was listening to while running through the Dutch countryside 10 years ago until I found myself lost in a cow pasture.

Ree and I are headed to Pamplona, Spain tomorrow night to participate in the festival of San Fermin. Well, not the whole "get drunk and dance to shitty Euro techno music," but more specifically, the running of the bulls.

About 500 years ago, some Spaniards got the bright idea to run in front of a small herd of wild and panic-stricken bulls to test their courage and show the world how absolutely idiotic they could be. Hundreds of years later, an overrated American writer wrote a book about this and exposed the world to the mayhem of this event. Eighty years after that book was written, a greasy-faced, insecure self-published writer from a dank basement apartment in Chicago decided to hop on a plane by himself and throw himself in the midst of the madness. He lived to tell about it. And giving fate the middle finger once again, he and one of his best friends are now planning on throwing themselves amongst the bristly and drunken faces of the crowd and the pointy saber-like horns of the bulls.

Because we have become accustomed to the deep ends of swimming pools.

Friday, July 6, 2007
3:02 p.m. A Beach in the South of France
❖

Ree and I are lying on our United Airlines blanket that we liberated from one of our flights. We are on an 8-hour layover in Irun, Spain but we walked for a while and ended up at a cafe in France. After lunch, we walked even more and found a beach on the ocean. There are titties everywhere. One might think it's just the old, saggy, nudist-type boobs, but oh no, they're legit. I act like it's no big deal but, "Whoa, tit-taaaayyys," keeps falling from my mouth and exposes my inner 14-year-old.

I often wonder if I will ever outgrow that 14-year-old. That dude is impulsive and obsessed with boobs. He is insecure and makes transparent attempts at arrogance that only expose his insecurities that much more. That dude wants as little responsibility as possible, so when the time comes to move to deeper pools, he doesn't have to disappoint as many people. See, because it is easy, and easy is the cousin of lazy, and lazy is the cousin of death.

But the view is nice.

Sunday, July 8
2:33 p.m. Barcelona, Spain
❖

Since we last spoke, I've taken a train from France to Pamplona, Spain for the Festival of San Fermin.

Last year, I was so singularly focused on my goal of running with the bulls that I was able to put the shittiness of the festival in the back of my head. I walked through the streets with my head down avoiding the Spanish taunts and drunken madness. Take Mardi Gras, the largest frat party you've ever had the displeasure of attending and the sports bars that adorn the 8th circle of hell, mix in some color coordination, a language barrier and a lack of showers, and there you have the Festival of San Fermin. Yesterday, as we were gathering our luggage, a red-eyed, English-speaking tourist who had recently been tear-gassed for being in the wrong place at the wrong time said, "I'm getting the fuck out of here, this place is a disease." Ree and I both nodded our heads in agreement. This was after we told everyone that Ree was a diabetic and needed to get to her medicine from her backpack then paid 20 euro to cut in the baggage claim line so we could get to our bus in time and get the fuck out of dodge.

Aside from the 2 hours of sleep on the concrete behind some bushes, we managed to experience 45 minutes of the most intense madness one can volunteer themselves for in their lifetime.

Before I left, people kept asking me the same thing, "Dude,

you did it last year ... why would you want to chance it again?"
I would always respond the same, "Because I still can."
While I did accomplish one of the goals on my "things to
do before I die" list, there was a small part of me that was a bit
disappointed that I played it too safe. So when I heard that Nyree
wanted to do it this year, I figured this was my chance to redeem
myself. So I did. I made sure to throw myself deep in the bedlam.
Instead of avoiding the crazed and panicked-stricken bulls, I got
as close as I could and yelled, "Toro! Toro!"
Is it idiotic if you are well aware of what you're doing?
I wanted to touch the bull. I wanted to feel the fear again. I
wanted to push my line. I wanted to do it right.
So I did.
Then I got hit.
Yeah, my dumb ass got a little too close and WHAM! Right
in the guts.
I put my arms out and the horns smashed into my elbows and
dragged all the way to my knuckles. I ended up in the air and
upside down. I managed to scurry away just in time, and the bull
went after some other rocket scientist. But still, I wanted to touch
the bulls more. I looked down and saw the thin rivulets of blood
rolling down my fingers. I needed more. More intensity. More
danger. So again, I went running back into the fire ... because
fuck it, why not?
Yesterday, luck and agility were on my side, and I was able to
escape with only a few minor cuts and bruises.

I feel redeemed. Last time I did it just to do it. This time, I
did it with my eyes wide open and a chip on my shoulder. I feel
good about it. Now I can truly say I don't feel any regret. Thank
god I never have to go back to that place.

Afterward, we peaced out and rolled out to Barcelona. Ree

left me for the airport, and I tried to find hotels. But it being summertime, I couldn't manage to find shit. I eventually got so frustrated, I walked around until I found the nicest hotel I could find and got a room. Not that I'm rolling like that but fuck, when you thought the Olive Garden was a "fancy restaurant" when you were a kid, if you somehow find yourself staying a couple days in Barcelona, Spain by yourself you might as well do it right.

I opened the doors of my room, and I stood on the balcony that over looked the Olympic square and exhaled. I turned and fell into my bed and slept for 12 hours.

Currently, I am sunning myself next to the rooftop pool listening to '80s George Michael. I love the fact that Europe is still really obsessed with '80s music, and not in an ironic way. It makes me smile, like you would at a little kid who gets really stoked at the simplicity of a tricycle or a piece of chocolate. You just want to pat their little head and say, "You're so adorable."

Sunday, July 8, 2007
9:47 p.m. Barcelona, Spain
❖

She has a way with me.
Booms and crashes and swoons and fucks.
I've never yelled "fuck you" at someone so hard and meant it so much.
Because she sets me off ... and someone who can't pull at the lows doesn't have a chance at the highs.

They.
They never shut me down. Never pushed me over. Ever set

me free. Ever fucked me so hard.

They never ran my car in the red.

I throw hate at her with my eyes because so does she. Because we both know we're in this together. Not in that "We're going down in flames" kind of way ... but in that "Holy fuck, we're going down in flames" kind of way.

We are clawing at each other's arms. We are wide-eyed and terrified. But no one sees what we see. Not even on their best days.

It's desperate and frantic.

It's filthy in the fuck, and it's villainous from behind.

It's whispers into shoulder blades and pushing words on to her neck so quiet and so deep, fuck, I want her bones to rattle.

She's my poison.

She's my fuel.

She's my street-walking cheetah with a heart full of napalm.

Oh yeah.

She has her way with me.

Tuesday, July 10, 2007
8:09 a.m. Frankfurt, Germany
❖

There is something so humbling about sleeping on the ground. While I genuinely despise being cold, exhausted and uncomfortable, it's like a jolting and miserable reminder not to get too big for my britches because I never know when this ride is going to end. Ever been on a subway when someone hops the gate and keeps looking back to see if anyone saw him? Looking over his shoulder, he walks briskly, not too fast to look guilty. That's me. The kid who got away with smashing the cop car window. The homeless man who walked into the restaurant and was greeted with a table, a smile and an ice cream sundae. The feeling of surprise and appreciation is constantly overshadowed with bouts of guilt. I keep looking around for a check to pay, but one never comes.

But it will.

Thursday, July 12, 2007
3:08 a.m. Hollywood, Florida
❖

Their eyes tell me they're mine. But more importantly, that I am theirs.

The words are projected from my mouth and into their ears, and I know, they're mine. And this time, it feels good. To know that it's for all the right reasons. Well, at least in my head they are. They get it. A room full of picked-lasts, forgotten, abused, tormented. I know this because if they weren't, they wouldn't be here in the first place. There was something, something that gravitates me towards them. Them towards me. For some, I've had twice as long to learn the rules of this fuck-you-up game no one teaches about in classrooms. They think I have answers. I tell them I don't. But they smile, tear up and swear to me that I do. So I ask them the question: the only question I know will make them question their loyalty to me. Because while I love, appreciate and hold their faith, I don't deserve it. Truly.

I pause for dramatic effect because that's what they do in the movies and it works.

"So, how many of you kids have learned how to swim when

someone threw you in a pool or a lake?"

There is usually a bit of hesitation because most people don't want to be the first person to raise their hand. But slowly, hands poke up. Sometimes a few; sometimes more.

I direct my question to those with their hands in the air, "And what happened?"

Pause.

"Um, I learned how to swim."

"Because you never knew what was in you until someone took you out of your comfort zone and forced you to do what you had always thought was impossible."

I let it sink in. If I speak too quickly the words will be lost. And I don't want them to be. I can't afford it. Because that is what I base my entire night on.

Because while I do it for me ... it's not about me.

It's about them.

She Said
❖

"I just want someone to understand me before I die."
She wasn't trying to be dramatic, nor do I think she was desperately reaching out to me to fill that void. I think she was just saying it matter-of-factly, out loud. She is a grown woman, with the same problems we all faced when we were goofy and ill-equipped teenagers. I wanted to say something that I thought might help, something from the old toolbox of quirky, yet witty one-liners that I have for such occasions. But nothing came to mind. So, like any 8-year-old kid when faced with a question or accusation he or she doesn't feel like addressing, I responded with another question.

"Well, what does someone have to do to make you feel understood?"

Appropriate question. One that might even cause someone dig a little deeper to get to that insecure buttery center, but truth was I felt the same way. Then I was overcome with sadness. I just wanted to just respond with, "Yeah, me too," then we would hug and find what we were looking for in each other, like two junkies.

But I didn't because I knew she didn't.

And she didn't because she knew I didn't.

So I wished her a "good luck" and went about my night wishing that someone would wish me "good luck."

Friday, July 13, 2007
11:24 a.m. Chicago, Illinois
❖

I landed in Chicago yesterday, and I was in no rush to get home. Went out for lunch and a movie. Going home felt like an end, yet also a beginning. Since I quit my "real job" at the salon, it has been just an overload of sensations. Airport to airport, town to town, country to country. New food, friends, fans, smells, beds, responsibilities, expectations, fears and loves. And every night when I stand on that stage in front of the handful of people who see something in me, I do my best to pull from what I have to give those people what they deserve. My biggest fear is losing the sincerity. So in bed, at night, I close my eyes, intertwine my fingers and relax myself into a kind of state that allows me to feel like it's just my bathroom mirror and me. I look into it and I say, "You can do better. You can love harder. You are not good enough." It's my tough-love regiment, and they get to watch. Because they deserve it. But it does a number on me. Late, after the antics are over and I find some place in the world to lay my head, it washes from me. I decompress. And it's emotional: to dig and pull at the scars and bruises night after night. To stand and talk about what my father did to me and the ones I love. About my lost opportunities. About my fears and insecurities. To pull from the bottom of that. Yeah, it begins to wear on me a bit.

And now I am home. To build this device back up. All eyes to the future.

All my life, I have never had a plan because I never wanted

a plan. I was aware that it was never my dream. The effort, the work, the hours, the school, the time clocks. It wasn't my dream. So why put in the effort? Why bust ass? Why look to the future? Shit, it wasn't *my* future so why the fuck should I care so much? Companies know that sooner or later people will come to that realization, so they create motivational seminars to convince you that you have made the right decision. Meeting upon meeting of, "You're doing a wonderful job, but ...," a pat on the back and a kick in the ass. For what? Whether I was honest enough to admit it, I was aware. I had enough. So with crossed fingers and a dream, I quit.

Now what?

Now I look to the future for the first time because I am my own best investment.

Now I believe in 5-year plans. Not to simply pay the bills but to maintain this life, this dream. To constantly evolve and progress. To tear away these hooks from mediocrity and to see what I can make of this package of bruises and bones.

And I'm wishing myself good luck.

Sunday, July 15, 2007
2:41 a.m. Chicago, Illinois
❖

I woke up at 8:30 a.m., crawled out bed and went to lie down on the couch in the living room. I stared at the ceiling for 3 hours. The alarm went off in my room, and I heard the groans and her clumsy ass knocking shit over in a desperate attempt to hit the snooze button. I jumped into bed and held her from behind. We fucked and she left. I went back to the couch. Lying there in my underwear, I just couldn't seem to pick my head up today. Day-after-Christmas depression. So much I've worked for and planned is now over and this is my time for rest but my mind cant stop thinking of moving and fixing and creating. I suppose that is a good thing, to constantly be progressing but you know, I would just like to breathe in and fucking relax. I laid there in my underwear until 5:30 p.m.

Eventually I showered and walked to Jim's apartment to eat pizza and watch "The Empire Strikes Back." Afterward, we walked to get ice cream. I met Jim years ago when we waited tables at the same restaurant. We also shared a friend, Dennis. Dennis is one of my best friends in the world, yet is currently dating my ex-girlfriend of 3.5 years. This recently came to light, and Jim asked me how I felt about it as we walked down Broadway Avenue and ice cream melted down my fingers.

"Well, fuck it, what can I really say, 'no, you cant date her?' That is the reaction of a selfish little brat."

I tell myself this so it hurts less.

"We broke up for a reason, I was never going to be with her again so fuck it. I love her and I love him, why wouldn't I want two people I love to at least make an attempt to build a happy life together?"

I do believe these words, just not so much at this moment.

"I won't lie, it hurts right now, but I know that it won't so much next month, then the next month, and after that it will hurt even less. Six months from now I'll be laughing at how childish I was feeling."

I know this because I've been here before.

But it is the truth. Time does heal all wounds ... if you love yourself enough to let it.

45

Wednesday, July 18, 2007
3:48 a.m. Chicago, Illinois
❖

Does it matter if you dig ditches or peck information into a computer or move shares or process insurance claims?

I mean, fuck; fuck the money. It's all just someone else's pittance.
Just the horse for someone else's cart.

The world also needs people who don't follow their dreams. Our society would collapse if it were run by a bunch of selfish "artists" who sat around drawing and painting, writing and playing music. A world of self-important assholes pontificating in art galleries, in the back lounges of tour busses and over black coffee diner counters.

Shit needs to get done ... but honey, I ain't your Huckleberry.

Thank god there are so many cowards in the world.

Monday, July 23, 2007
6:25 p.m. Chicago, Illinois
❖

The impression I have gotten is that the older you get, the more intelligent your decisions become. By that reasoning, one would come to believe that the people you choose to surround yourself with would be better for your soul. While this isn't entirely false, the one thing that becomes clearer with time is that we begin to take on more responsibilities and the rigors of life compound. This leaves little time for me. And sure, it is about me, why not? Why should I feel guilty to see life as mine? For all I know, when I close my eyes at night, the entire world disappears. If Chris falls in the woods and no one is around to hear it, does he make a sound? As long as I don't careen through life stepping and crawling over people to find my happiness, as long as people aren't negatively affected, should I feel guilty? Well, dammit, no.

I feel myself slipping into that place of comfort ... no, laziness. The one that compels me not to go running, to sit on the couch, to lay around at night zoning out into the television, watching the lives of others while electricity is roaring through the streets.

There is so much I need, but I am too lazy to go get it.

There are no losers. There are only people who gave up too soon. And I can feel that pull into mediocrity, into contentment. I can feel my bones creak and my eyelids grow heavy. My lungs don't have the capacity they once did, and my tolerance for stupidity gets a little shorter every year.

But I know this. And that is the one thing I have on my side. The knowledge that something is wrong.

And there is far too much world out there for me to be sitting on my ass.

It is time to get moving.

She Said
❖

"You know, you and your friends with all of your tattoos and fighting and fucking ...

You guys know how to love.
Fuck, you really know how to love."

Wednesday, August 27, 2007
1:57 p.m. Chicago, Illinois
❖

You know, I've been thinking about how a majority of my anger comes from disappointment.

I don't know, maybe I expect too much from people. Well, I don't think that's exactly correct ... I think I may expect people to react too much like myself in certain situations. Do you know that almost every single holiday/birthday I've celebrated with a girlfriend has ended in an argument of some sort?

So, why are you so neurotic, Chris?

See, it really does take a lot to upset me. Seriously. But it doesn't take much to disappoint me.

Examples:

I dated this girl a while ago. She liked me because of what we would talk about as we laid in bed together at night and stared at the ceiling in the dark. I loved this time with her because she loved to listen, and I loved to talk. She wanted to know all about every dark corner, and I was more than willing to tell her every and anything. She was attractive and had amazing breasts. I do not lie. But see, the problem was, on her birthday I surprised her at work with flowers. She wasn't stoked. That bummed me out. Hard.

Call me selfish, but I was bummed because I felt she never truly appreciated any of my boyfriend-type gestures.

And no one feels good when his or her efforts are unappreciated.

53

Another girlfriend, for her birthday, before dinner, I took a detour to pick up this jacket for her that I had specially ordered to surprise her with. She told me that she didn't want it because she knew I couldn't afford it. Fuck, I wouldn't have gotten it if I didn't want her to have it. I wanted her to have it because I knew how badly she wanted it when she looked at it online, and I wanted to be the one responsible for her happiness. I played it out in my head, you know, that she would geek when she saw it and I how I would respond to her enthusiasm. Instead, she got mildly upset. We drove to dinner jacket-less, and I stared daggers at her over stuffed mushrooms. I tried not to let on how disappointed I was because, shit, it wasn't my birthday. The one-day that's actually NOT about me.

And that's it. They don't respond the way I would. Friends, family, boyfriends, girlfriends. Maybe because they see the world in a different light, I understand this. But you know, it doesn't make it any easier for me to accept. Childish, possibly.

In all of my years searching, I think I've gotten it all wrong. It's not about the music you listen to, your sense of humor, your boobs, your tolerance of my antics or how you look in the mirror.
It's about appreciation.
And in the countless nights of whispered indiscretions spoken to dark ceilings, not once has it felt reciprocated how I ever play it over in my head.

Thursday, August 28, 2007
8:31 p.m. Chicago, Illinois
❖

And when I get home, I return to my hermit-like state. If not for the calls and texts, I wouldn't leave this moist apartment. I retreat back to the safety of my bedroom where I dream about watching old science fiction movies all day. But it's light out and I need to let the sun know that I appreciate it. So I force myself outside. Then the calls and texts begin, and I'm guilted into dinner somewhere because that is what my friends and I do. We eat. Often and in large quantities.

But I've always liked to be alone. I think this surprises people. I like sleeping alone; I like traveling alone; I like sex alone; I like lying on a couch alone and I enjoy eating alone. I've always maintained that you have to learn to be your best friend because you never know when someone will leave or die. But somewhere along the way, I think I've become far too dependent upon myself. Some days, I feel like a social shut-in.

"The Day The Earth Stood Still" is playing on the television in my room in five minutes. I will be there.

Alone.

Thursday, September 6, 2007
6:25 p.m. Las Vegas, Nevada
❖

I don't gamble because I'm bad at math.

I don't go to strip clubs because they're a waste of money.

I don't go to clubs because I can be pretentious and arrogant without a $20 cover charge.

And I don't drink because it's a waste of time, money and brain cells...

So why do I love Las Vegas so much?

It's Disneyland for adults.

I won't lie; I find comfort in prostitutes and drug dealers holding up streetlights. It reminds me of that desperation that I left behind in Chicago. It's in the eyes of the terrified rats on a sinking ship scratching and clawing to save what's left of their bottom feeder life.

It's real and raw open sores.

And you have to respect that.

Monday, September 10, 2007
11:30 a.m. Salinas, California
❖

I understand the beaten. I can see why they have given up. I know this now, and while it puts things into perspective, it also helps me understand the lives people choose.

Rich, poor, young, old, skinny, fat ... none of this matters.

What does matter are the coping skills we have been taught. If no one teaches you how to deflect the shit that gets thrown at you, some of it will start to stick. After a while, you may actually believe that you deserve a shit-covered life. And I see those zombies. I've worked with them. I've given them change. I've loved them on vomit-soaked couches in roach-infested apartments.

Every day, I look into their eyes and see them covered. Covered in shit. I want to run up to them and grab them by the shoulders and ask who it was that didn't love them enough. Who that adult was that let them believe that the shit was real. I try to tell them that the shit is not real. That I know this because I believed the lies as well. The shit that sticks to us, weighs us down, holds us back, spoils relationships and ruins dreams...

It's not real.

It is the sum total of every last irresponsible adult's insecurity.

Because when that shit gets so heavy that it begins to weigh people down, they panic. And like the small people they are, they look for the vulnerable. The weak. The ones with the largest target on their backs. The children. The abused. The left behind. The left out ... and they throw. With all their might, every last word that they know will stick the best because that's what the adults before them did. And that's how they get ahead, get up, move forward ... by stepping on the weak, the trusting, the people who don't know the pain of being a victim. They push down and step over.

But there is another way.

Wednesday, September 12, 2007
1:04 a.m. Mill Valley, California
❖

Today is the first day in a while that I've been worried about money.

I don't live lavishly. I never have. Mostly because I've never had the opportunity. But this year I've put out two books, and a little money came from that. I got all confident because my bank account rose to four digits of extra money, so I quit my day job. I figured I could survive touring from town to town with this new life, running my mouth in front of a room full of kids. I don't charge admission; I ask for donations and sell merch. But right now, it's barely covering my costs and I'm getting worried. I don't want to go back and give up on my dream. It's all or none but those figures keep getting smaller and smaller. Returning to my old life wouldn't be a cowardly decision, it would be a sign that my dream is slouching toward it's inevitable death, tough for a kid who makes a living off of writing and speaking about living his dream.

Car rental, gas, shitty hotels and even shittier food begins to add up quickly, and on the Southern leg of my recent speaking tour, I made a $57 profit.

I don't want to say it's about profits. I want to say it's about the love and smiles I see and the friendships and appreciation I receive, but love and smiles don't keep the lights on.

I'm worried. For the first time in months, I'm worried.

But I have to keep my head down and keep moving forward. I have to. Because I've promised myself I would give this my all.

100 percent.

Because I never have before. For anything.

And this isn't a job or a girl or a class ... this is the first thing I've ever believed in.

Now let's just hope it believes in me.

We Were Kings
❖

I never knew how to fight.

But that was all he knew.

He didn't fit in and he listened to the same bands I did. I knew it from the T-shirts he wore. Our peers scorned us both for our inability to "go with the flow," so we bonded. Our love for self-loathing was only surpassed by our loathing for the ones who walked the halls looking down their noses.

We sneered and made childish generalizations about their status amongst the high school pack of sheep.

Together we were solid. A unit. No one thought like we did. We were dethroned kings; waiting for the day we were to regain our title. Because, see then, then the chicks would see that we were more than the flash of leather jackets and Sid Vicious sneers. We would be revered for our individuality and our sense of originality. But until that day, we had to keep our eyes to the ground while we awaited our rightful place.

He would spend many evenings at my house eating microwavable burritos and shooting at whatever wildlife mistakenly stumbled into my backyard. Calling girls, watching soft-core porn and listening to Misfits bootleg records. We came together at the perfect time. The planets aligned and we met … and we skated the same ramps, listened to the same music, went to the same shows, and we understood that we were kings. We bonded even more over the similarities of our broken homes. He had an absent father and a mother that didn't understand. I had an absent father and a mother that didn't understand as well … but the problem was, my mother tried to understand.

This he resented.

When I was inclined to point fingers to those I accused of stealing my rightful place, my mother did her best to diffuse that anger. But no one was there for him, so that anger went into the mirror ... and when you're a teenager and you hate yourself, it's only a matter of time before that anger is directed outward. I watched as it built.

First it was the preps that ruled over our lunchroom.

"Those fucking sheep," he would say under his breath, as they would walk by.

"Why do THEY get the hot chicks?"

I would frown and nod my head in agreement.

Then it was the suburban gangbangers that ruled the halls.

"Fucking fakes. Like any of these kids could even point out where Compton is."

I would frown and, again, nod my head.

Then it was the blacks.

"Fucking blacks, why are they so fucking loud?"

That was when it struck me that this might be headed in the wrong direction, but again, I nodded because I didn't like what I saw in the mirror as well.

"Fucking Mexicans, they come over here and steal all of our jobs."

"Whoa dude, I'm Mexican," I responded.

"Yeah man, but you know what I mean. You're cool because you're not like a 'real' Mexican."

This wasn't the first time I heard this phrase, nor would it be the last.

As time went on, rhetoric like this became commonplace. It began as petty as punk vs. what we viewed were conformists, but soon racism, homophobia and bigotry were the excuse and reason for whatever it was that was missing in our lives.

And I bought in...

To an extent.

Because I didn't fit in. No matter how much I tried, no one ever liked me for me. I was always too skinny, too dumb, too small, too "gay." There wasn't a direction for my anger. There was so much that when I dared to look it in the face, I ended up taking a razor blade to my skin, or breaking out the windows of cars, to telling my mother to "shut her face" because that animosity had to go somewhere ... and when you're young, the sights you've been given aren't calibrated for shit.

So I aimed,

And shot,

And hit all the wrong targets.

Soon I began to see the holes in his reasoning. The figures and statistics he would throw at us during our skate sessions in the street now ruined our fun and were beginning to wear on us.

He blamed blacks for welfare and drugs.

He blamed gays for their supposed lack of morals and for AIDS.

He blamed Mexicans for the lack of jobs.

And he accused the Jews of controlling the media and blamed them for the death of Jesus.

He blamed and he blamed. He pointed his finger, accused, tried and convicted everyone that wasn't like him. Everyone that didn't live his life. I may have been young, but even then I saw that he had turned into what we hated. What we stood against. What we espoused to never become.

I didn't want it anymore because hate is heavy, and I was too smart to actively seek out such an unnecessary and overbearing burden.

So I took one of the most important steps in my life. Standing in front of my bathroom mirror with clenched fists and a tear-streaked face, I asked the question "WHY?" over and over.

It hurt, and it was scary.

It was like picking at a scab, but I knew it was for the best.

One evening, in the bathroom, I learned that I can't control the lives of others, no matter how much I hate. The only control I have is over myself and I wasn't even doing that well. How could I possibly point fingers, accuse and hate people, cultures and communities I didn't know when I didn't even understand the kid who looked back at me in the mirror?

I had no right. I at least learned that much that evening, that I had no right.

Luckily, what else I learned was that I had an obligation to myself to be as brutally honest as possible because I knew that if I couldn't be honest with myself, that I would never have the ability to do so with anyone else. And how was I supposed to learn how to love and BE loved if I couldn't stand naked and alone in an empty room? I was sabotaging my own life by attaching the insecurities of others to my back.

That night I promised myself that I wouldn't live a life that only moved forward to push others down.

I never had many role models in my life.

No teacher that went the extra mile. No coach that got me through hard times. No tutor who helped me make the grade. No priest who taught me how to love. No godparent that gave me the secrets on how to allow myself to *be* loved.

But that's fine.

I've had enough people in my life to show me how NOT to live.

And that's all the guidance I need to learn how to be a king once again.

Friday, September 14, 2007
2:46 a.m. Flying above the United States
❖

I walk into rooms and see the faces, and I let them control me. They don't know it but they control my speech, my volume, my patterns, my humor and my ease. I take jabs at myself because it sets me at ease. Because, maybe if I tell them I'm not worth it, they'll believe it, as well, and I won't feel the pressure of expectation.

But I've never lost a room.

I have never walked away with regret or relief. The only regret I've ever felt was that I didn't have enough time to give even more of my soul away.

I've never lost a room.

I wish I could believe in myself as much as they do.

Thursday, September 20th, 2007
11:21 a.m. Batavia, New York
❖

We laid in bed last night after driving for an hour or so. I spoke in Buffalo last evening. The coffeehouse was far too small so we moved across the street to a park. The setting was nice. Me, my book, about 30 people, all under a tree. Hugs. Smiles. Pictures. Thank yous.

Afterward, we drove to some shitty hotel and laid in bed, using our computers. We both had aspirations to attend to. After an hour of silence, she looked over to me and said, "You would think by now I would be sick of hearing the same stuff over and over again."

For the past two weeks, she has been in the back corner of every venue taking notes and giving me constructive criticism. Sometimes I don't project well enough. I need to work on more background for the story about my father. I say "you know?" far too often. I sniff my snot, and that's gross.

"But I'm not."
"Really?"
"Every time I hear a story, I take something new away from it."
I wish she knew just how many of these stories and rants were directed toward her. Were inspired by her. I held in my victory-smile and nodded.
"I don't know, something about what you were saying right before you told the marathon story tonight ... I don't know, it ... inspired me to go after what is going to make me happy in life."
I wanted to hug her but I know who she is. She's stubborn and skittish and sometimes you have to admire the beauty of feral animals from a distance. If I went in to hug her she would see that I was getting through to her ... and since she is still a folded-armed 13-year-old girl with an attitude the size of Texas, well, sometimes I have to be humble with my triumphs.

So I didn't smile.
I didn't hug her.
She buried her head back into her computer and put her headphones back on.
And me?

I'm actually beginning to believe in myself.

Sunday, September 23, 2007
1:06 a.m. West New York, New Jersey
❖

Again I find myself looking out the window from New Jersey to New York across the Hudson River.

The ferret and I are at Mikey and Alicia's apartment watching The History Channel and listening to their pets mosh around the living room. As much as I want to geek and hug and kiss them, I'm so tired that all I want to do is lay down and use one of the cats as a pillow.

You would think this tour wouldn't take much out of me. I drive, get out, walk into a venue, grab a bottle of water, stand on a stage and spill out my insecurities to a room of my own personal therapists. I've learned so much about myself simply because I get the opportunity to have daily sessions and uncover more black spots in my brain.

The kids think I'm up there to entertain them ... but really, they're there to listen.

I hope they never notice.

Tuesday, October 23, 2007
9:42 a.m. London, England
❖

Last time I was here was during an 18-hour delayed flight layover. I didn't get to see much but the inside of buses and cabs, since the tube stopped running at 10 p.m.

London has always held a certain mystique to me. Some kids need night-lights to fall asleep. When I was younger, I needed the movie "Sid and Nancy."

I loved looking at the buildings and thinking about the generations of people that have inhabited them. The streets always looked so romantic, the dark and dismal cobblestone alleys: it all looked like a movie set. Until I got here and realized that the people in this city live on a giant sound stage.

My flight arrived around noon yesterday, and I made my way via tube to my room at a bed and breakfast. Similar to Elwood's room in the movie "The Blues Brothers," my room is 6 feet by 4 feet, which is actually smaller than my bathroom back home. As I'm typing now, my head is resting against one wall and my feet are propped up against the opposite wall.

When I'm on tour in the states and I'm in a new city, I always wonder if anyone will show up. It still strikes me as odd that people would want to see me. That I say nothing new and all of my ideas are stolen from people who have said the same thing so much better. I don't know. All I've managed to come up with is they like my delivery. They tell me why they come, but I'll never believe them.

Yesterday, when I walked down the stairs I was surprised by what I saw. A full room of people waiting quietly and patiently. I've been off for about a month now and it took me a bit to find my footing, but after the first 10 minutes I got right back in my groove. I don't like the time off; I feel the rust beginning to creep up. The kids here are wonderful, and I want to marry each and every girl so I can keep that adorable little accent for my very own. Something about the crowd last night was different. I feel like they were more involved. As if they saw past my smoke and flash and history and really dug into my stories during the question and answer period. They wanted more background, more insight, more of a painted picture. I loved it. I didn't want it to stop.

Afterward I went out for fish and chips across from Victoria Station because like Jim says, "You gotta do 'the thing' when you're in that town."

Fish and chips is definitely 'the thing'.

Wednesday, October 24, 2007
10:48 a.m. Nottingham, England
❖

I get the impression that they take me a bit more seriously over here. It has only been two dates into this short UK tour, but already it's a different atmosphere when I walk into the room. They listen more intently; they ask the questions I always wish people would ask after I empty my guts into the air. Ones that call into question my motives and shows me that people really are paying attention. Shit like that keeps my wits sharp. Telling stories about rubbing my penis on girls and answering questions about my favorite color does not challenge me. Even their "thank you"s sound different; as if they are appreciative of the art and the vulnerability.

Last night was a bit more casual. Some days it's just more difficult than others to go to the cellars of my heart and open the caskets of the past to a room full of strangers.

Some new friends and I went out for food at the oldest pub in England last night. Established in 1185, knights in armor would stop by this place for a pint after a long day of murder or pillaging or whatever it was that knights did. I couldn't wrap my brain around the fact that knights came in here for a bite of food with a sword by their side, like it was no big deal. And now there was this arrogant, lazy American sitting in their seat eating an apple pie.

Saturday, October 28, 2007
12:56 a.m. Glasgow, Scotland
❖

We talked and she congratulated me on taking chances with my life and I smiled and said I was happy that she was doing well with her new relationship.

I'm still not too sure if that was a lie.

She asked if she could ask me a question. An opening that always evokes that sense of dread. It only seems to preface an uncomfortable and clumsy question, in addition to wasting seconds of my life asking a question about if you can ask me a question.

"You know how you say that the person you date is a direct reflection of who you are, what you love and what you're willing to tolerate?"

Yes.

"Well, how do you justify it when you call her an asshole?"
I countered with adjectives like:
Spontaneous.
Unpredictable.
And intelligent.
Which she is ... that along with being an asshole. So, I suppose I get what I deserve.
I deserve her.
I am realizing that she's the first woman I've ever felt like that with. It's like I've been searching for so long to look someone in the eye, but every person I've come across is either a roach or a giant. And I've always seen her as a roach ... but she's growing. No one seems to see that but me. She's a tough-ass street kid with concrete eyes full of "fuck you," but she's chipping away at that mountain of rage with desperate fists and revealing a more beautiful person. That is what I want people to know. That it's not how you look out of the package, but what's revealed after crawling through the grit and grime of your past. That is real. That is what we are. That is what is more attractive than it all.
I'm in love with mile 24 of the marathon.
The last minutes of the Titanic.
Lust. Infatuation. Stalking.
It is passion.

Common people live common lives and their love is safe and easy. They are civilians in my world and I need soldiers with chips on their shoulders down to fight and die for the cause.
And she's got that in stripes.
Common is boring. Something she has never been accused of. Boring never tore into it. Boring never scaled walls or grabbed lovers by shirt collars or pulled my hair so hard that the pain crossed the line into pleasure.

My Nancy Spungen with the dented heart of tin.

But see she's feverishly laboring away, knocking out the scrapes and bandaging the scars and attempting to gold plate that motherfucker.

That is why I'm in love with an asshole.

Monday, October 29, 2007
1:41 p.m. Norwich, England
❖

I've painted myself into a corner.

Thank god.

I never thought I would have the courage.

"Living well is the best revenge."

Middle fingers to the sky.

You may win the war but the battles for hearts and minds are all mine, fucker.

I want them to feel my hands on their throats.

My nails carving my name in their chests.

It doesn't have to end in slow decay.

Rage and rebellion are alive for as long as the time you give them.

It sickens me when I watch people murder their light by living lives that steal love, cross lines of compromise and crash down on their heads. What's even worse is that they believed it when someone told them that they didn't have the strength to hold it up.

To carry the load.

To break it apart.

Suicide bombers without targets.

Decades of preparation for what? To step on the mines of tradition, planted by ancestors who lost the map?

Traitors to the very god you worship.

You should be ashamed of the time your mother spent on her back, bleeding and pushing.

No one is proud of birthing cowards.

Hollow smiles. Hollow hearts. Hollow love. Hollow love.

Do you love like a coward?

How do your friends feel? Do they feel loved?

Are you doing all that you can to make her feel adored?

Do you deserve to be loved?

Do you?

What have you ever done to make yourself more lovable?

Hopefully later than sooner, god's going to kill me.

But I'll be damned if I don't leave a good punch-up behind.

Tuesday, October 30, 2007
4:12 p.m. London, England
❖

The interviewer asked if I ever considered writing fiction.

"I only know how to talk about myself."

Shit, can't I stop being an ugly American for one goddamn second?

"What motivated you to write?"

I said what I usually say because it sounds better than, "I don't write, my fingers are simply obnoxious ego-maniacs."

I told her I'm a story-teller.

What I really wanted to tell her is that odds are she is a better writer than I am and I wish the camera was turned around so I could pick her brain and scavenge the pieces of her education that she's still paying off. That I am simply a boy with a chip on his shoulder, waiting for life to take its shots so I can strike back with my paper alter ego. That I've compromised my soul by stocking shelves for companies I loathed. That I've waited on customers with a smile after being called an asshole. That I've jumped inside garbage dumpsters because the boss told me that I wouldn't have a job if I didn't. That I've hung my head and walked away from street fights like a coward.

I wanted to say this, watch her face and look into her eyes to see if that spark of awe remained.

Friday, November 2, 2007
6:45 a.m. Chicago, Illinois
❖

I woke up at 6 a.m. to watch the sun rise over the buildings downtown.

There is an amazing view of the skyline from her 3rd story window, and my internal clock is still telling me to go drink tea.

I wonder if life goes on without me.

Tuesday, November 6, 2007
11:05 a.m. Fairborn, Ohio
❖

I don't like coming home in the middle of tours, I lose momentum. I return to couch-mode and two days isn't enough time to fall out of love with touring. While I enjoy the decompression, I seem to plan my travel just when I begin to hate my apartment.

On my lonely drive from Chicago to St. Louis the other day, a goose committed suicide by diving into my windshield. Scared the fuck out of me. There I was, minding my own business when this asshole the size of a goddamn Beagle throws its body into the passenger side of my windshield. I screamed, "HOLY FUCK," then realized I couldn't drive another three hours to St. Louis with a shattered windshield. Luckily, I always pay the extra money for full coverage insurance for just such events. I canceled that night's speaking, filed a police report, hopped in a tow truck and rolled with a meth-faced driver, while he chomped down a gas station hot dog in silence, to the airport to promptly exchange the rental car.

I hate canceling speakings because I can't handle the guilt of disappointing people. One of the few things that hurts my heart. I just think of the people that baked me cookies or wrote me letters or spent gas money to show up to an empty room. People that want to be in the same room as me. I still don't understand it and I certainly don't want to make people regret their energy. I bums me out hard.

I've been trying new things on this tour. For the past year I've been telling so many of the same stories that they work well for me. They flow because I've worked them over so many times. Which is good but gets boring for the audience. I have to remember that in the end, I am an entertainer. So I've been telling stories I've never done before and I try to do some impromptu rants toward the end. I really like it; it keeps me fresh and alert and reminds me that I don't have to work from a mental script. Some people trust in my words, so why shouldn't I? I keep falling into the "easy" trap. It's so warm and comfortable, like milk and cookies or toe socks in the winter. But like I've always said, easy is the enemy. Sure, I can cut through that parking lot when I'm running, because no one will ever see. And sure, I can tell the same story about my father and my encounter with the bulls in Pamplona, Spain, but who am I really cheating?

Tonight I will try new stories. The first few times are usually shaky and awkward. I pause too much to catch my footing and do my best to remember what comes next, all while fighting my ever-dwindling memory to keep all the details accurate.

Last night in Indianapolis, after I told my stories, I began ranting. I never know what direction I will go in. Sometimes the words that fall out of my mouth surprise the shit out of me.

"It's not ok to hate yourself," I said.

After I said it, I paused. Not because I was unsure of where I was heading, but because I realized that I was not telling the room as much as I was telling myself.

"It's not cool to hate yourself."

I see so many forums out there that openly embrace self-loathing. How fucking disgusting. Maybe I just never gave too much thought to the music and the words and the art. Of course it's entertaining, but like looking at a steaming pile of dog shit, it really isn't moving me forward, revving my gears or allowing my wounds to heal. If anything, it's counter-productive.

"Feeling sorry for yourself isn't fucking cool."

I wondered if the audience knew that they were watching evolution right before their eyes. Under the lights was a boy making progress. The desperate strokes of a drowning boy reaching for the edge.

I wonder if they saw it.

She Said

"My friend has had a life like yours, but she said that in her stories there is no inspiration to be found."

I said, "The horrors are as inspirational as you let them be."

Sunday, November 11th, 2007
11:30 a.m. Salem, New Hampshire
❖

Recently I've been getting e-mails accusing me of "changing." That I'm "not the same person" as I was four years ago.

I smile and say, "Thank god."

Wouldn't it be terrible if I stayed the same? If I was the same arrogant and insensitive prick I was years ago?

I think some of the kids mistake evolution for change.

What so many people seem to misunderstand is that you have the option to grow old. It's not inevitable. It's a choice.

Look around; you can see it in their faces and hairstyles. You can note the era in which they refused to embrace evolution, when they made their stand and said, "No more progression for me, thank you very much." Because evolving, continuing to explore, taking risks, stepping outside of that comfort zone takes effort. And as you grow "old," effort becomes more and more difficult. So they stop. They wear the same hairstyles and claim that music nowadays sucks because they don't understand it. They believe rebellion is best left for the youth. That's when they grow old; when they rust. When they walk up to their pre-determined hole or their ass and willingly place their heads inside.

Change is when you believe your own hype. When you allow the forces against you to affect the course of your life. When you sacrifice your art. When you crawl over people to get a piece. Change is a lateral move. One without purpose or direction.

Evolution is forward-thinking.
It is a strength gained from the uncertainty of progress.
And clarity that only comes from taking giant unaided steps into traffic.
Fuck change.

Evolve.

Monday, November 12, 2007
5:31 p.m. Montréal, Canada
❖

I'm sitting in my car right down the street from the coffee shop because I hate showing up early for my speakings. I don't need a grand entrance, but when I walk through the door of the venue and I don't see anyone, a mild panic sets in. See, my single biggest fear is to do a speaking and no one shows up. I have absolutely no fear of speaking in front of crowds. None. I've had people yell "asshole" at me in the middle of one of my most emotional stories, people give me the finger, I've had to speak outside in 100-degree weather while two different bands blasted songs over my voice, and I have yet to lose my footing. But it's those few minutes after I push open the door and walk in with my suitcase of merch that I feel determines my confidence level that evening.

I've never done any speakings in Canada. Today at the border, they seriously got in my ass. They ran background checks, tore apart my rental car looking for god knows what, Googled my name, found my Livejournal and Myspace pages and proceeded to read all about my life while I sat in the waiting area, trying to not look nervous. After an hour they finally decided to let me into their country, only after telling me that they could seize all of my merchandise because I didn't claim it nor did I have a work permit. The man handed me back my passport and license and said, "but we like your message." I doubt they would have said the same had they lurked a little more and found some of my peepee stories.

I haven't felt well in days. I get dizzy when I stand up quickly, I don't have much of an appetite (yet I haven't lost any weight), I have serious bags under my eyes and I can't keep any food or drink in my body for more than two hours. Good thing I'm all alone in my travels or I would seriously turn off anyone sitting next to me from town to town. But I've come up with a saying that gets me through it all:

"What would Black Flag do?"

After reading, "Get in the Van" by Henry Rollins, I've realized I can never again tour and complain without a twinge of guilt. They toured with no food, no money, constant fights, stolen gear, closed venues and sometimes no one showing up to their shows. I can't imagine the blows they took to their morale. And while it truly is about those 90 minutes a day I stand in front of crowds, my level of morale determines the quality of what comes from my mouth. So I need to suck it up, keep my chin up, be thankful that anyone has walked more than 10 feet to come see me and open up my chest and hold up my heart like it was my last night on earth.

Just like Black Flag would.

Time to go to work.

91

Tuesday, November 13, 2007
5:19 p.m. Ottawa, Canada

Again I'm sitting in my car in downtown Ottawa waiting it out before my speaking. While I was driving here through vast expanses of barren fields, I turned my iPod off, shut down my phone and got to thinking about this old hardcore band called Brother's Keeper. They would play Chicago every few months to lackluster crowds. They were good enough, but the thing that kept kids coming back was what the singer Mike Ski had to say between his screechy songs. You could feel his sincerity. I had never seen such brutal honesty. He cared so hard for a scene of kids and a philosophy of life that his voice would crack between songs.

"These songs aren't about slogans and dancing hard. You have to take the message here and apply it to the real world."

I remember it vividly. While everyone cheered, I saw those same kids walk back into the "real world" and continue the same self-defeating behavior. Like what? That was what they meant about people just "not getting it." I saw it and it made sense. I genuinely wanted to try and make myself better. What did you do differently? Show, don't tell.

Any band can play their hearts out in a small and sweaty room for little to no money. They do every day. But to have substance, to say one line that can resonate in this little brown motherfucker years later ... those are the rooms where I grew up. Those are the rooms that still do make me think and call my intentions into question. In those rooms is where I learned that it's not how good you do in the eyes of others but how good you do compared to the dude who looks back at you in your bathroom mirror.

And I've got some promises to keep.

Brother's Keeper broke up years ago. I still see Mike every now and then when he tours with his current band the A.K.A.s. He's a solid dude. Solid. I know he looks back at those glory days with pride and nostalgia. I just wonder if he realizes that one phrase he uttered on that 2-foot tall plywood stage at the Fireside Bowl over 10 years ago is still alive in some kid's head. That this kid still thinks about that day and what it meant. This kid didn't see a simple singer of a band but a mentor that opened a window to a world of no return, which is fine by me.

I grabbed that moment, held onto it like a newborn to a blanket and haven't let go.

Sunday, November 18, 2007
2:06 a.m. Chicago, Illinois
❖

Night before last I spoke at Utica College in Utica, New York. Smaller crowd, but I had a stage and an auditorium. I like a little stage so I can see people in the back, but not so much that I don't feel like I'm a part of the crowd ... because, if anything, I am a part of them. Afterward, I drove from 11 p.m. until 6:30 a.m. through the snow and darkness of New York, into Canada and cut through to Detroit. While I was attempting to cross back into the states, the border patrol officer barked at me, "Open your trunk."

I looked in the rear-view mirror and saw as he walked behind the car, went into the trunk and started rummaging through my boxes of merch. He closed the trunk walked up to my window and said, "So, why do you have so many copies of the same book?"

I said, "They're actually mine. I'm a bit of an author."

He paused and said, "Really? Um, I'm a bit of an author myself."

"Really?"

For the next 10 minutes, I found myself talking books with this massive border patrol officer with a 9mm pistol strapped to his side, which I couldn't stop staring at. Odd.

At 6:30 a.m, I finally landed at the house of one of my best friends in the entire world, Gheesling. She and I met online, strangely enough through some of my writings. She insulted me and I called her names; we never stopped talking since. She comes from my polar opposite world: corporate job, house, nice car ... you know, responsible adult stuff. She is an amazing person. Funny where you find allies. I had an early speaking outside of Detroit in Ferndale, one of my favorite places to speak. I've been here many times before, it may be the first place where what I do began to catch on outside of Chicago. Every time I'm here I feel like I'm in a room of friends. Today, on two hours of sleep, I walked into AJ's cafe on 9 mile road to an eruption of the "happy birthday" song. I couldn't stop smiling and felt a lump in my throat. There are so many good kids that show up in this town. Not because of who they think I am but because of who they *know* I am. A big group of genuine motherfuckers. An artist couldn't ask for anything more. After the speaking and post-show hangs, I hopped back into my rental car with the last speaking of the tour completed.

Five hours later, I pulled up in front of the ferret's apartment in the Ukrainian Village neighborhood of Chicago and honked my horn. She hopped in my passenger side seat and told me to drive to LU-LU's, which very well may be my favorite comfort food of all time. Located in the not-so-great area of Ogden and Western on Chicago's West Side, it isn't too far from where I saw my first drive-by shooting. My mother and father would take us there after visiting my grandmother in the area when I was a little kid in the '70s. I loved it; it was the one thing that I actually looked forward to on those weekends. Their hot dogs were and still are perfection. I re-discovered LU-LU's years ago when I mistakenly found myself driving through the wrong neighborhood to get to a show, and I saw the little white building. A rush of emotions came flooding back, and I made a U-turn because I wanted to see if the hot dogs were as good as I remembered. Now I go at least once a week. The place hasn't changed since I was still too short to reach the counter. The same yellowing pictures of local celebrities hung on the wall. Players from the Bulls and the Bears, newscasters and mayors. Jokingly, a few months ago, I was standing there waiting for my food when I turned to the ferret and said, "Honestly, no bullshit. If I could get my picture on the wall here ... I would consider THAT 'making it.'" We laughed and talked about how amazing that would be, to grace the walls of our secret spot.

Tonight, we pulled up in front, got out of the car, walked in and ordered our regular food. The ferret looked to me and asked, "Do you mind if we eat here instead of taking it to go?"

"Sure."

We walked into the dine-in area and there was a small table closed off from the rest with a little blue happy birthday table cloth draped over it. I thought it was cute, thoughtful and quaint.

I smiled and asked, "Did you do this?"

She smiled back.

We ate our food, then the owner of the place walked up to our table with a cake. I laughed. I thought it was the most adorable thing ever. While eating our cake, the owner approached again, pulled out a black frame, set it on the table in front of me and said, "And we would love it if you would write a little something so we could hang this on our wall."

I looked down and there was a framed picture of me from a speaking. My mouth hung open, I couldn't believe what was happening. I looked up and he handed me a pen. I looked at him, cleared my throat and said, "You have no idea what this means to me."

He turned to the ferret and said, "She's the one that made this happen."

I've gotten my fair share of gifts over the years, most I don't deserve. But tonight, I was so taken aback; so overwhelmed that someone would go that extra step for me. I felt guilty for every moment I didn't think she had the capability to be a caring and giving woman. She made my night. She made it. I hovered over the picture for at least 15 minutes before I came up with:

"To LU-LU's. I am honored to grace your walls. Christopher Gutierrez. Author. Friend. Customer since '78."

Simple. Just like LU-LU's.

When we went to leave, he took the picture and hung it above Mike Ditka. I didn't feel like I deserved it. Even now, as I write while the ferret sleeps next to me in her one-piece footie pajamas, I still continue to smile. Not only because I see her growing into a woman, not only because my picture hangs in my favorite little restaurant in the entire world but because now, at the age of 33, I have had the best birthday of my entire life.

I'm home from tour with a big toothy smile.

Wednesday, November 28, 2007
3:46 p.m. Chicago, Illinois
❖

She woke me up four times screaming last night. I sometimes wonder if I have the capability and tolerance to keep nursing her back. It's been like this for months. A few days here and there will pass without incident, but overall, it's nine out of every 10 nights. Sometimes the terrors are small, and I can diffuse it by whispering in her ear, "It's ok, it's just a dream."

Most nights not.

Most nights she won't wake up unless I gently rub her awake. On and off since we've met, I've come to learn what works and what doesn't. Talking to her doesn't work, she screams over me. Yelling her awake just makes her more upset. Grabbing her arms while she thrashes about in her sleep only startles her awake and immediately she thinks I'm trying to rape her.

I have to catch it before *he* gets there, in her head. That's what she tells me. Last night, I failed. She woke up swinging with her eyes closed. She yelled his name. She swung at me and missed. She sat up and kicked at me in the bed like she was fighting off an attacker. Him. He made it in her head last night. I know because she screamed at the top of her lungs, "HE'S HERE!"

I tried calming her down by carefully placing my hands on her shoulders while whispering, "He's not here. He didn't get you."

She collapsed into a fetal position, hands over her face, back to me, sobbing.

I held her from behind and told her I was sorry that I couldn't save her from him.

It's such a contrast to who she is. Strong, abrasive, tough exterior. She's been punched, kicked, raped, overdosed, stabbed and left for dead. I know because she tells me ... no matter how much I don't want to hear it. But I learn about her and her past. I finally told her I couldn't handle any more. I can't hear any more stories. I told her I don't care to know anymore about her past and that I judge her based upon the person she presented to me the night we met, that the past indiscretions matter little to me. If it doesn't affect us currently, I don't need to know. I don't need to know about the abuse. I only need to know about the person she is and the person she aspires to become. I told her that there is no reason to tell those who care about her the terrible, terrible things of her past. She told me she needed to tell someone. I told her it doesn't have to be me. She asked why. I told her because those stories hurt the ones she loves. She just stared at me. I asked her, "Why do you want to hurt me? Is it because you want me to hurt like you hurt?"

She sat silently until the tears came to her eyes and said, "I never thought about it like that."

Last night, I held her sobbing and sweaty body until her cries faded into whimpers and she fell back asleep for the fifth time; I thought about how much a plane ticket to where he lives would cost. I was wide awake so I played out the scenario in my mind. I have time off before the next tour. I could easily disappear for days and no one would notice. I could fly into his state, rent a car, find his house and wait. I have nothing else to do. I wouldn't kill him but I would and could beat him within an inch of his life. The police would think it was random. There would be no motive or suspect because no one knows what goes on in my dark bedroom at 4 a.m.

When she wakes up, I tell her about the evening before and she remembers nothing. I tell her I put the blanket under the door like she asked me to and she asks why. I say, "Because you told me he was looking under the door for you."
She tells me that's what he used to do. I ask her about him. She asks me how I know his name. I tell her, "Because you scream it at the top of your lungs every night."
She doesn't remember the punches she threw or how she yelled, "Get the fuck off me!"
Because to her, I wasn't Chris. I was him. I let myself become him because I wasn't there fast enough to save her.
She hung her head and said, "How sad is it that I'm 29 and I still have a boogey-man?"

It is truly amazing the amount of harm so many adults inflict upon children and how we spend the rest of our lives suffering from and learning to live with tiny moments of filth from our past. What's worse is that we are doomed to repeat to our children what people have inflicted upon us. It's been that way since ever since because so few possess the ability to break that cycle.
I wish I could make her pain stop. I have learned how to carry my load over the years. It wasn't easy but I've re-arranged it so I can walk through this life comfortably, or as comfortably as I allow myself. I want to carry hers. I can do it, I really can, but she wont let me.
I don't want to fix her...

I only want her to want to fix herself.
That's all I've ever asked of anyone.

Thursday, December 13, 2007
12:36 a.m. Chicago, Illinois
❖

I'll tell you a secret. I've always loved watching women sleep. Everyone reverts to a child-like state when they sleep. So innocent. So peaceful.

The stress of work compounded with awesome television, it seems like I never get to hold them the way I truly want to. Like intimacy is only reserved for sex and handholding at shows. And while I'm very open with my affections, I play the game too. Because like .38 Special said, "Hold on loosely, but don't let go." Hold on too hard and you run the risk of smothering, and no one wants that guy. The weak and spineless gropey PDA guy. It's a delicate balance.

But at night. When they breathe heavily and slobber up my pillows, I hold them with every inch of my skin. I whisper sensitive artist drivel in their ear and I kiss them over and over. Because at that moment, they are mine. They are ideal. No inhibitions.

I wish I could do this with eyes open, but the rules of the game don't work like that. So I give enough for them to know that I still love hard but not so much to scare them off. And at night, when no one is watching but the cats, I hold them like you held your pillow when you were young.
I hold them hard.

Away Messages During Long Silent Drives Home From Indiana Strip Clubs

❖

It was the way her mouth moved and pushed out sins that drove me to infatuation. One might have thought that the sting of wonderment would have faded, but to the dismay of my old and rusted heart there she was, still my oasis. She pushed through the black-light night, half-naked, spilling, "Fuck you, cocksuckers" into the dark club. Her skin shimmered, her hair smelled of smoke and her soul had been beaten by the misgivings of dirty old men ... but in the end, she was mine. All mine.

Life-Rattle
❖

When people ask me what my biggest fear is, I usually say, "wasting time."

That I've wasted years sitting on couches, zoning out into a video game or a situational comedy, absorbing nothing significant and wasting everything. My years of being raised in a Catholic family by a mother who seems to have taught the church everything it needed to know about guilt trips, hasn't really made things easy on me, as well. It's not that she would tell me that I was wasting my time, as much as it was the tone in her voice and her wide-eyed expressions when she would say, "Um, ok Chris. If you wanna quit your job, that's fine by me." This is a fear of mine. A huge one. A fear that I won't go out clawing and scratching to accomplish what my heart tells my hands they need to feel. To grasp and hold against my chest. To learn and kneel down to share with my niece, Gianna. I've wasted years of time. Years of good life. But honestly, that's not my biggest fear.

My biggest fear is that I will lose that deep eye-fluttering intensity for what is most important. That my arms will get heavy from reaching toward the sun and I will dilute my words and actions with shine and flash to take away from the fact that this soul is getting old and tired. It's sad that it takes moments in books and minutes in movies to evoke heart-swells and life-rattles.

My biggest fear is that I won't know how to stop that fog

from seeping in and taking over. From stealing the light from behind my eyes. I see the lifeless. I see them every day. I watch as they stare at sidewalks. I listen as their relationships reduce them into what they never thought they would become. I watch as they perpetuate the cycle their genes have known all along as they turn into their parents, inflicting the same crimes they have always preached against.

I write this out of a fear that I will become my father. My father's mistakes. My mother's guilt and regret.

I write this out of a fear of mirrors. Because I fight it every single day. It's not something I like to talk about because it is difficult to admit that you're afraid you're losing it. The fight. The true desire to become. To become something, anything.

Because I see it in the people who resemble my father.

Them.

The ones who burned away their potential, gave up the race and threw in the towel.

They have become a part. Rank. File. Common. Not common because they're "civilians," common because they turned their backs on their desires, ambition and appetite.

I need to become beautiful.

Become remarkable.

Become unforgettable.

Become someone's everything.

I don't want a life without lust.

I need to crave. To yearn. To hunger.

We work our being and burn daylight, for so much that we forget that the greatest investment is in ourselves. That we are the answer to our own problems and the only reason why we are not taking the steps to heal is because we slowly let that fog creep in, choke out our devotion and block out our internal sun. Our desire.

And when we leave our desire behind, we have no chance to break the cycles we are doomed to repeat.

But I've still got a few rounds left in me.
And a desire to fight.

And that's all it takes.

Something To Fight For

❖

"Why won't you just fight for me?" she pleaded.

I was letting it all go.

Five years.

Minutes before, we were lying in bed completely content, unaware, staring at the 4 a.m. ceiling.

"So I was watching 'Oprah' today."

Oh, here we go.

"This woman stood to ask a question, and Oprah asked who the gentleman sitting next to her was, and she said that it was her fiancée. Oprah asked her how long they've been engaged, and she said 11 years. 11 years!?!"

She paused, understanding the gravity of her next statement.

"I don't want to be that girl."

She had every right. I knew it. Five years of movies, dinners and holding hands at shows. See, that I can do. It's that whole entertaining a commitment for the rest of my life thing that makes me uncomfortable to the point of nausea.

She turned her body toward mine, propped herself up on one elbow and stared at me, waiting for a response. I had none.

"I just need to know that I'm in your future," she said.

"I don't know." I wasn't being one of those obtuse douchebags who shied away from emotional confrontation. It was the truth, I simply did not know.

"I'm not asking you to marry me now, I just need to know if you have plans for us in the future. After five years, I don't think that's asking much."

And it wasn't. I knew that. We were best friends. We laughed and rarely fought and fit together well on the couch. It was simple, but it was good. Solid. And here she was, throwing monkey wrenches in my easy and comfortable suburban punk lifestyle. Another way to say it would be she was forcing me to take a good look at myself and the direction of my life. What were my intentions? Because I certainly didn't have any. It took years to realize that it never was about her; it was about my own fears of becoming a man. I always feared what I viewed as "adulthood." I thought that saying, "Yes, you are in my future" would set into motion a series of events that would undoubtedly leave me castrated, harmless and comfortably seated in front of a television for the rest of my life. "Husbands" never dove off stages, threw snowballs at houses or ate greasy food at 3 a.m. diners with friends. They never made much of a fuss or asked their wives for permission to spend their own hard-earned money, and they looked forward to their upcoming Home-Depot weekend. And that's what that simple, shaking little boy felt when his girlfriend stared at him for a response. Because I still had life bleeding out of my eyeballs. Granted, I was still too insecure to wield this power but fuck if I was going to let anyone take away my options. I believe that is how most men reluctant of commitment see it; that women are forcing them to make a choice, because see, there is comfort in options. Options allow people to daydream. To envision themselves leading productive, meaningful and adventurous lives.

Banksy once said, "Nothing in the world is more common than unsuccessful people with talent."

But I would amend that to, "...with talent and options."

Because so many people fear making that choice, that decision ... because it instantaneously dissolves the remaining options. And what if you made the wrong choice? Took the wrong path? Fuck, think of all that wasted time and effort, nevermind looking foolish to my friends and family. I mean, I only have one shot at life, right? It's much easier to lay here with a girl who would never question our future, *my* future, and never dare to ask that I pick up my shit and make a goddamn decision. No, I would rather lie here looking at my 10 fingers and know there is comfort in those 10 options. What I didn't realize then was, most people die of old age staring at those 10 fingers.

Without breaking my glare at the moonlit 4 a.m. ceiling, I said, "I love you. I do. But I don't know if you're in my future."

"I think I deserve a yes or a no," she said.

"I couldn't agree more."

"So which is it?"

"I don't know."

"You don't know if it's a yes or a no, or you don't know about me being in your future?"

"I don't know about you being in my future."

I knew what I was saying. They were the words that break girls' hearts. The only thing I could hope for was that she would respect my honesty and not punch me in the throat.

"Are you sure that's your answer?" She was giving me a chance, a way out. To backpedal. To save this. To make this real. To take a risk. To hold out my heart, like she was doing for me.

"I'm sure."

"Ok. I think I should leave."

She sat up in bed and stared at me. This was the point in the movie where I was to lunge forward, hold her by the back of her head and pull her forehead into mine while nervously whispering, "I don't care what it takes, I swear I will make this work. You are the love of my life, and I cannot lose you."

But I didn't. I laid there like a coward, as she glared at me with incredulous eyes and sighed in disappointment.

She got out of bed, walked over to her clothes and began getting dressed. I just laid there in silence, as she slowly began picking up her belongings.

"So this is it?" she said with tears looming in her eyes.

"I think it's for the best."

She stared at me in disbelief as if I had just punched her in the gut. With tears in her eyes, a quivering bottom lip and an expression that was more confused than upset, she said in and angry and high-pitched voice, "Why won't you just fight for me?"

That did it. That kicked a dent in my heart. Not simply because I was physically and emotionally torturing this wonderful girl who rubbed my back and believed that I was actually worth fighting for, but because until that moment it had never occurred to me that I had never fought for anything in my entire life. And here she was, the most wonderful girl I had ever known and I wasn't willing to claw and fight to do whatever was needed to save our five-year investment. I was disgusting and low. I wasn't worthy of her love and I knew it.

She turned and walked out.

I walked over to the couch, sat down and put my head in my hands. I began to sob. But like the selfish fuck I was, it wasn't about her. I felt alone and abandoned. But the night's events shook my insides and forced me to think about my future. One that I had never entertained. But I swore, that night sitting on that couch, I swore to myself that I would use this opportunity to make a choice, to look at those 10 fingers and choose one. Choose a direction and choose a new life and never again waste anyone's time on a heart that wasn't willing to fight back.

Years later, Andrea went on to date my best friend, of 20 years, Matt. When I found out, it immersed my heart in acid. I felt my body convulse and heave forward. I punched and kicked at no one. I snarled my teeth and proclaimed to the walls that I would never let another soul in. That no one would get in deep enough to do damage.

Recently, I was the best man at their wedding.

It took months of talks, a stiff upper lip and a good long look in the mirror to stand and hug Matt. It took everything I had to calm my chattering jaw and say, "All right man, you better marry that chick and make her happy."

And he did.

And he does.

And when I was handed the microphone and stood up at their wedding, my hands shook uncontrollably. Not because hundreds of people were watching and waiting for what I would say. But because my best friend and a girl whose heart I broke years ago were sitting next to me.

I pulled a piece of paper from my tuxedo pocket and read the following:

"Matt is my innocence.
From Catholic school CCD classes to
Cheating on tests to
Playing ding-dong ditch to
Skateboarding in the streets to
Discovering girls to
Avoiding street fights to
Jumping ramps to
The awkwardness of adolescence.
I have seen it all.
And I have watched him grow.

We have secrets. Secrets sworn to never be told to another living soul.
And he hasn't.
And I haven't.
We have history.
A history more memorable and visceral than I have with people who share the same blood as me.

We have a bond that time nor distance cannot break.

And we have bombproof promises that have withstood decades.

We have watched, as like watching mirrors we have turned into men.
Men that people never expected.
That people counted out.
Men that have learned to love, respect and honor.

This man, right here has watched me grow as I watched him grow.

Andrea is my guide stick.
The first person to not only tell but SHOW me how to do right.
The first person to show me how to love.
The first person to call me on my antics.
The first person to teach me compassion.
The first person to explain to me how important LISTENING is.
She is tolerance, understanding and empathy.
Everything that my best friend matt has the ability to nurture and appreciate.

Andrea floats when she walks and is grace personified.

I never had a real father.
No one to teach me how to throw a baseball.
No one to show me how to change my oil.
No one to tell me when to stand my ground.
No one to tell me when to let it go.
No one to show me how to throw a punch.
Tie a tie.
Negotiate a raise.
No one to show me how to EARN anything.

But this guy, this guy did.

You see, matt is my father.
He is a true guiding light, one that leads by example and a man who truly understands that relationships are a gift and should be treated as such.
He is the man to which all others are measured.
He is my hero.

I am proud to call him my friend.
I am honored to be in the presence of such absolute devotion.

Together they beam light. They are living love.
The kind of love you dream about.
The kind of love you close you eyes and wish for three times for when you're a kid.
The kind of princess you hope to rescue and they type of prince you pray that saves you.

I understand, because I know them well.
And I know how well they love
And I know, just how well, they know to love one another.

I'm not here to wish you luck.
You don't need it...

Because you've ready won.

This. Right here ... this right here is the real deal.

And I say this with the utmost sincerity and conviction...
You're the best I've ever known."

I set that paper down and with a lump in my throat, I turned and hugged Matt hard and said, "I love you."

I sat down and realized that was the first time I was ever willing to fight for something. I loved him and I loved her ... but I wanted to believe. Believe in *this* heart. Mine. That it was strong enough to take that stab, that punch to the gut and not only make it out of the burning house alive but to stand and raise my hands to the sky and scream, "How can you ever learn how to fight for someone when you don't even know how to fight for yourself?" The fight to live is the only real love you can ever feel for yourself and there isn't anything you cannot do if you love yourself. So fuck it, like the saying goes, "The best investment is in yourself." It was time to believe that I was worthy of a real life and real love and visceral emotion. I was worth it.

Oh, but it wasn't that easy. I had to hear it one more time. Those words.

"Why won't you just fight for me?" Kate cried out.

I sat across from her on the couch, and I couldn't believe that I was hearing those words again.

"I ... I just think it's for the best." How could I have let it happen again?

Another one, Kate. Again, wonderful and stunning but after years of making choices, sprinting for goals and taking risks, I was tired and looked for comfort, and she was warm buttermilk. She wanted a future. She wanted security. She wanted what I didn't have the ability to give. We fell out of "lovers" and fell into "friends." We both saw it coming but when she said those familiar words, again, I was at a loss. I hung my head and felt the sting of embarrassment. That I had lost sight. I wanted to tell her that I can't live up to what her kisses and messages promise. I can't make it worth it. I want to tell her what a mistake I am. That my love isn't nearly what they dream of or what their mothers ever wanted for them. That I am fireworks with bum wicks. All promise and no flash. But self-deprecation is the easy way out. It's the mark of a coward.

I couldn't fight for her because I couldn't love her the way she deserved. I didn't have the capacity. I still needed to explore and discover. To learn the difference between "needing" someone and "wanting" someone. To find faith in my ability to make and keep someone happy. To test my limits and reach for goals past my reach, so that one day I could believe that I have earned people's love.

Instead, I hugged her, kissed her on the forehead and walked out of her apartment.

Months later, my other best friend, Dennis sat me down and told me he was falling for her. That he couldn't help it and he wanted to let me know before anything progressed. He told me that it was important that our friendship survived and that he wouldn't do anything to jeopardize that. I smiled that kind of smile that you do when you're at a loss for any other expression. It wasn't an easy smile. It took everything in me from slamming my hands on the table and screaming, "Why are you doing this to me when you know how badly I hurt last time?"

But I didn't. Because it was time to let go of the past. No matter how hard you try or how badly you want to hold on to yesterday, it's just that. Yesterday. Never to happen again. You either progress or regress from yesterday. And it's not about what you've done, it's about what you're doing. Kate was in my past, Andrea was in my past. They are yesterday. Dennis and Matt are my now. I love them and they love me. I know this because they tell me, show me and make me feel loved like I deserve to be loved. They are the greatest people I've ever known. Kate and Andrea are wonderful women with the potential to make someone happy for the rest of their lives. It is selfish that I would want to keep them apart. I needed to let go and embrace their happiness. Letting go isn't about them as much as it is letting my old self go. Letting the jealousy and immaturity evolve into compassion. Being ok to go on with life, without setting up my own roadblocks and pitfalls. For all the faith they have put in my ideas, my ridiculous head, and me … I owe them. I owe them the same honor and reverence they would give to me.

It's easy to be selfish, jealous and hateful.

It's difficult to be open and compassionate and to allow someone a shot at happiness.

It's easy to hold onto the past and retreat back into warm couches and simple relationships.

It's difficult to fight for ones you believe in and who believe in you.

And that was when it hit me. There is a difference between "earning" faith and "deserving" faith. I need to earn hearts. That is how you learn to love yourself. By letting go of the selfishness. By stopping the blame. By accepting the responsibility that while the hearts you've been given may weigh heavy, you are blessed to have such burden. Because so many people walk this earth easy without that weight and will never know the happiness that comes from the strain of the journey and the words, "I believe in you."

That's when I realized that the only heart you really have to fight for is your own.

The rest just fall in line.

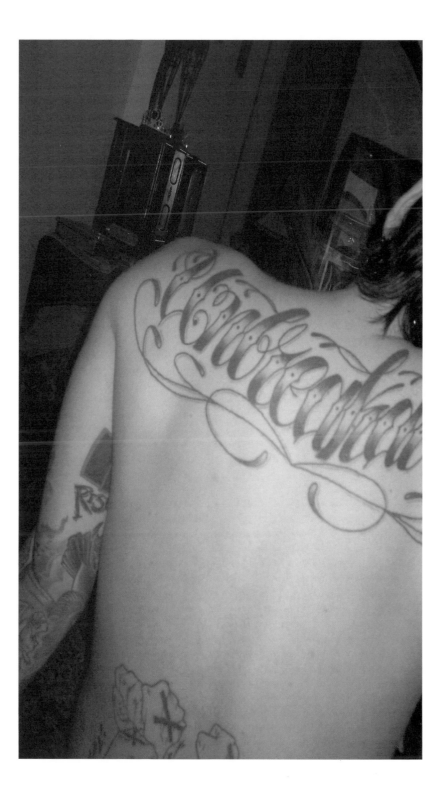

Saturday, January 12, 2007
9:17 p.m. Muncie, Indiana
❖

At 9 a.m. yesterday, I hopped in a van with five friends and began my first speaking tour supporting a band.

Andy, Dan, Pete, Justin and Dave make up the local band 2*sweet. I've been friends with most of them for years, knowing them from the Chicago hardcore scene. Months ago, we came up with the idea for me to do a short supporting tour with them. The idea being that maybe we could turn some new kids on to each other. I also figured, shit...I wont have to drive, worry about getting to places on time or do long sets of new material. I figured this would be an easy tour for me, but truth be told ... it's a bit awkward.

Last night was my first show in Minneapolis, although I think it went over fairly well, and I managed to get most of the upstart rowdy kids on my side, by the end of my 20 minutes, I just didn't feel "in the zone." Usually, I recount a story from one of my books but since that's like the old shit at this point, I want to do more of my upcoming stuff. More personal, more rants, more opinionated. I began incorporating more of that into my last tour and it was received well enough, but what I didn't consider was that on this tour, the majority of kids at these kids were there to mosh and get out their aggression in an unsupervised atmosphere. Hey, I guess that's what "punk" is to younger kids. That's fine, I guess. At least I'm getting that animosity out in a mildly productive manner and maybe some where along the line a new idea sneaks in their heads.

Sometimes I look back at touring with longing eyes and forget how much mental effort it takes to travel across the country. Being a writer who looks forward to rooms of people who want to be there makes those days of being in a band that no one wanted to see seem so distant that they almost don't exist. Like all those hard memories just became good story fodder and what remained were the good times.

I'm on tour opening for bands that most of the people in attendance don't even want to see ... so imagine how stoked they are when some dude who they only see as "riding the coattails of some band" walks on the stage. Oh yeah, here's 20 minutes to change minds and try to get kids to pay attention to my little after-school special "message."

I don't miss being in bands trying to win over ungrateful kids. But I have a newfound respect for them. I took for granted all the people who came out and sat in front of me in coffeeshops. I've always loved them but whether it was 5 or 100 kids who showed up, I could at least depend on the fact they wanted to be there.

Not on this tour.

I wish I had the energy and insight to tell you it's moments like this that build me up after breaking me down. That shows with "fans" are easy and don't require as much passion because you know you don't have to pry open minds. But right now, while curled up in the backseat of a van at 1 a.m. in the darkness of Middle America, it's difficult. It's difficult because it makes me feel like I'm regressing. And I wonder if I have the steam to keep chugging back up and over the hills of Pennsylvania.

I sat behind the merch counter today, which was next to an open garage door, huddled amongst T-shirts and hoodies, hood up, gloves on, hoping that one person would buy something, anything. I sold one CD and one DVD. $25. Then the promoters didn't want to pay us so some amazing kids who felt bad that the show they tried booking for us fell through gave us $65 to split between me and 2*sweet. I only took $25.

I wish I had the conviction that is required to get through every night knowing I am exactly who I need to be. Who I am. Who I aspire to become. I can do it most of the time, yes, and truly believe it. But you show me someone that says they've never had second thoughts and I'll show you the world's biggest liar.

I won't give up.

Chris, you won't give up.
Promise?
Promise.

Monday, January 14, 2007
7:17 p.m. Blairsville, Pennsylvania

It's so easy to stay positive when things are going well. When you're secure in your relationship. When you're in a good school. Good job. When you genuinely feel like you're going somewhere and working toward something. But when the show's over and the sex becomes mechanical, when you get fired and dumped and overlooked and unappreciated ... well, that's when your real character shines.

It's easy for me to stand in front of crowds who want to hear me. My thoughts. My ideas. Me.

I always seem to be talking about my constant fight with easy. See, I crave it. I long for it. On days when I sit behind lonely merch tables with the efforts of the past 2 years laid out in front of me, I long for couches, pizza and familiar breasts. ~~It's cold and smoky and I need to take a shit.~~ I have bags under my eyes because the floor I slept on last night under the pool table wasn't very comfortable. The amount in my bank account is falling faster than it's coming in, and I feel more uninspired than I have in years. I would love to blame this on seasonal depression or B-market tours in the winter or women who don't understand how I need to be loved. But it's simple. It's not easy. And no good art ever came from easy. I wish I was writing, knowing this would make for an interesting blog or book entry. One that I could look back at in years and laugh at the insecurity that I felt was so momentous. Truth is, right now, at this very second, in Pennsylvania, on this snowy and freezing night at a sparsely attended show on a Monday night, it is real. I feel like I'm 5 all over again and I've lost my mom in the grocery store. Is it going to be okay? And really, I think that's all anyone ever really wants to know.

The kids are not all right.

Wednesday, January 16th, 2007. Portland, Maine

Maine is cold in the winter. Who knew?

I wanted lobster because "you gotta do the thing," so I asked employees and customers at the local Dunkin' Donuts where the closest place to get decent lobster was, and they looked at me like I was covered in feathers. One person finally spoke up and said, "Red Lobster." I should have punched him in the ear. That's like coming to Chicago and asking for pizza and getting directed toward the fucking Pizza Hut.

I spoke long tonight and felt like I finally had the complete and undivided attention I usually get on my book tours. I felt good for 40 minutes. I lived like I should. Sitting on the middle bench in the van, I counted my merch money. $69. I made nothing on the door.

God, I wish I could live on intentions and attention.

Thursday, January 17, 2007
8:33 p.m. Providence, Rhode Island
❖

A girl's mother tapped me on the shoulder after the speaking last night and said, "My favorite part in your speaking was when you said, "I don't drink, I never have. It's not my thing.'"

She went on to tell me about how these are the kids that really need to hear that kind of stuff.

I knew what she meant.

The lost.

The have-nots.

They were the ones who "needed" to hear those words. I smiled and nodded, but I didn't quite agree. I said that it wasn't so much the "drug-free" speech they needed to hear, because I've been the kid on the other end with those words coming from an out-of-touch adult. It all just sounds so distant, so far-removed from what high school life really is. Up to that point, it is the most stressful and intense time in life. Cliques and pressure and rejection and the desire to be liked, loved and accepted. Parents, teachers, jocks, preps, punks, detention, suspension, kissing, gossip. Fuck, I get it. I completely understand why kids steal vodka, smoke weed, huff paint, hate their families and want to take weapons into schools. All ill-equipped, awkward and questioning their sexuality and dealing with that thing in their pants, all while hoping that no one stares at their acne. To have some disconnected asshole jumping back and forth, using catch phrases that make you feel icky all over like when your parents try to be "hip" and "izzle" everything out is fucking insulting. Assholes think that by telling kids to "just say no," they're making some kind of difference when, in fact, if they knew shit about shit they would understand the effect of being told not what to do by adults.

Hmm, let's see. "Christopher, don't burn stuff."
Um, ok.
3rd grade, pulled out of class for attempting to burn down the school.
"Christopher, don't steal."
5th grade pulled in the back room of the local convenient store while police were called.
"Christopher, don't break shit."
"Christopher, don't vandalize."
"Christopher, don't touch the vaginas."
"Christopher, don't dive off the stage."
Telling a kid to stay away from drugs is as naive and as effective as telling a 4-year-old kid not to eat the cookies and then leaving the room for six days, no matter how bad you say they taste. Kids don't have coping mechanisms yet, and too many don't have responsible people in their lives that even take the time to push them in the right direction or instill them with confidence.

"Adults" don't see that this shit is bigger than a slogan on a T-shirt or a 70-year-old rich white lady on television or a hired gun in a school auditorium. It's not about telling kids to stay away from drugs. It's about making kids love themselves enough to know they don't need to hide from their emotions. It's about making your kids feel ok expressing themselves. It's not about telling kids they're going to hell because they make mistakes. It's not about belittling their problems simply because "they're kids." It's about giving them a forum to express their frustrations.

"Adults" that brush away the legitimate concerns of children crying out to be loved and understood by saying, "Oh, you don't know what you're talking about. You're just a kid."

Or

"You'll understand when you're older."

Just makes it worse.

I wish I could grab these insensitive self-important assholes and scream, "This is a life. One that you have a direct influence on. One that you can make better or make worse with a hug or a smile. Right now you have the ability and responsibility to make this world better by holding that little motherfucker's hand and showing that despite how fucked everyone else is, that they can swim against this tide of human swill to become bigger' faster and stronger than any human alive if they are simply given the opportunity to learn to love themselves."

No, it's not an ideal notion. The fact that "adults" believe it is, is exactly why so many kids doubt themselves.

I told her that it wasn't so much speeches about staying away from drugs as it was relaying stories of hope, compassion and achievement despite the odds and showing them that I'm just like them with my zits and insecurities, all while still learning how to deal with that thing in my pants.

Because drugs have one purpose: to shield your heart from pain. And if we can reveal to kids that our hearts truly are indestructible, they won't need another slogan or T-shirt or asshole preaching on a stage.

And maybe then we can finally make this a better world to live in.

Sunday, January 20, 2007
4:17 p.m. Driving through New Jersey
❖

We stopped at a gas station last night to get sandwiches and macaroni and cheese. For some odd reason, many of the gas stations on the East Coast have awesome mac and cheese, so Dave made us pull over. We walked in and put in our orders at the mini-deli they had. There were two people working the midnight shift. One guy behind the cash register who looked like the stereotypical janitor from some '80s slasher movie. You know, the slow kind of spastic drooling guy with knots on his face and too many forehead wrinkles.

Andy ordered his sandwich, and I began asking simple questions about the ordering process to no one in particular. Then, from behind the counter I heard a loud and irritated sigh. I looked up to see a woman who struck an uncanny resemblance to my sister, Cassandra. The combination of slicked-back dark hair, olive skin and slight chola makeup made me take note, but it was the attitude that really pushed it over the top. I asked her about the type of breads they used, and some incoherent mutterings came from her mouth as she looked up to the board that hung above her that described the breads as if she couldn't have been more annoyed. I just shrugged because really, I don't know what is going on in someone else's life so why get all bent out of shape because some stranger doesn't treat me the way I would have treated them? While we were waiting, Andy looked over the counter and whispered in my ear, "Whoa, finger tats."

Referring to the tattoos she has on her fingers that showed through her clear gloves. My little sister has a small tattoo on her

128

hand that she covers up, a remnant from her days of running with a group of hoodlums. Andy got his food and walked out, and I just stood there staring at this girl. This girl who could have been an identical twin to my younger sister. I couldn't tear myself away from watching her work. How this could be her. My sister. Then I began to think how humbling this job must be for her.

Nothing shows someone's petty character more than taking the piss out of a stranger based upon what they do for a living. Fuck, you don't know what has happened in their past or in their family that has forced them into that position. Oh, and how these small motherfuckers believe that their luck and opportunity make them any better than the fry cooks and waiters of the world.

All I can see when I look at her is what I know. She's a short-tempered woman with bad make-up and finger tattoos.

But she's fucking working.

She's not out robbing houses, dealing drugs or stealing cars. Well, maybe she is during her spare time, but let's be honest, anyone who's out there making that kind of ill-gotten cash probably isn't willing to waste their party nights hanging out in a gas station to serve mac and cheese to a bunch of loud assholes from Chicago for $7.25 an hour.

There's something to be said for people who have the humility to hold down minimum-wage jobs when the option to make money in other, less respectable ways is so much more appealing of an option. Not only for that 16-year-old kid selling your drunk ass tacos at 2 a.m,, but especially for the adults who have children or parents who have fallen ill or to make ends meet because the "man of the house" up and left to do blow and bang hookers.

As she packaged my food, I felt myself choke up. I wasn't sure why. I stood and watched her and at that moment, whether she wanted or even deserved it, I respected her more than anyone in the entire universe. It was midnight in nowhere America in an ugly gas station, and she was making me a sandwich with finger tattoos.

I know many people with finger tattoos and I know how humbling handing me that bag of food must have been. That wave of empathy rushed from my throat into my eyes and made them water and I looked at her in the eyes and said, "Hey ... thank you very much."

She casually looked at me and said, "Thanks."

"Have a nice evening," I said.

She ignored me.

I turned, walked out the door and looked upward to make the water run back into my head and thought about what it takes to live her life and keep her moving forward.

I stepped back into the van and wondered where she would end up later that night.

And the night after that.

She Said
❖

"Man, is it shitty out tonight."

We drove northbound on Lakeshore drive. Snow was blowing fast and horizontal across all four lanes of traffic. I looked out at the white nighttime sky that fell over Lake Michigan and watched as the massive waves crashed upon the concrete trail that runs along the perimeter of the lake.

"Yeah," I paused to smile, "perfect night for a run."

"You would say something like that."

"I run because I hate it so much."

"Sounds like a metaphor for our relationship."

I'm sure I could have responded with my usual smart-ass remark, but instead I stopped smiling and concentrated on the road ahead.

I didn't say much because I knew she was right.

I run because I hate it. Because my lungs burn, my legs ache and the wind pushes me back. My daily staring contest against my will. To prove to myself that I am better than myself. It's a constant test and trial.

Am I better than I've been told?

Am I better than I believe?

Am I better than I was yesterday?

Do I still have the stamina to push through the slush and snow, ice and rain, sunburn, chaffing and heat exhaustion?

It's everything I hate. It's uncomfortable and physically demanding and the results it produces aren't even all that noticeable. But fuck it. That's why I do it. I have yelled, "FUCK YOU," at the wind more times than I can count. I like that I hate it. It's a desperate combination of will, hate and heart that makes my jaw clench, my fists ball and my eyes squint as icicles form along my eyebrows.

She is the exhaustion whispering in my ear, "Just stop. Stop because you don't have it in you."

Sometimes I wonder if that is why I am doing this. Why I am maintaining this race. If it is, I don't need you to tell me that I'm doing it all wrong, because I know. But I'm not sure. I mean, where is the line between "the good fight" and being too dumb to stay down in the 10th round?

She is by far the most difficult task I've ever taken on. She makes my jaw clench and my fists ball, yet the results aren't even that noticeable. I feel unappreciated, insignificant and altogether misunderstood, but is that why I stay?

Is that why I fight?

Or is it because when the waves stop crashing and the snow stops blowing that I can see the beauty and brilliance in the trail?

That when she lies next to me and I look at her face, like I'm doing right at this very second, I feel inspired. That, I know that without a doubt, she would take a baseball bat to someone's face to protect me. That she is so violently loyal that I can see in her face, without a hint of hesitation, that nothing would make her happier than to have the opportunity to annoy the hell out of me every day for the rest of her life. Or maybe it's because I see the same fight in her eyes, only hers is more focused. She believes in her fight.

And maybe that's what I see behind her eyes, that she is the conviction I've been searching for in myself.

I need to figure out why I run this race.

Truth In Lending

I often wonder if we are all assembled with the same capability to hurt, crush and dash or if this is a learned behavior. Are we built like this? Do we learn this or do we unlock the demons that have laid in wait, dormant, sleeping until we have the balls or cowardice to awaken this destructive behavior?

I don't know why I do.

Sometimes I think it's better that way, because if I knew there was a precise moment, one that I could pinpoint, I would spend the rest of my years in regret. Just another thing to add to the list. Sometimes ignorance truly is bliss. But I can't help picking at it. Wondering, asking why, why do I do?

It's like the "Seinfeld" episode where George doesn't want Jerry to walk up and talk to a woman because he knows jerry will become "one of those guys." The kind of guys who can do. It's a line that once crossed, there is no return from.

I was fine until this damn notion of putting myself into uncomfortable situations to learn what I was truly made of came about. Just like everything else in this world, you have to take the good with the bad.

Awakening from a self-induced life coma, pulling my head from the pillows, grabbing the back of her hair to bring her in for a kiss, first steps in foreign countries, taking risks, calling shots, putting it on the line. Fuck, yes I know this is good for me, I do. I am happy with the life I've built. One comprised of real dreams, youthful ideology, vigor and fury. I am a lucky dude and I do not take this for granted, but I have also been given a life I do not deserve. I'm ok with that. Because fuck if life doesn't take it out of your ass somewhere else. Oh, trust that the universe doesn't let you get too far ahead. It always catches up to you, asks for its share for the house and reshuffles the deck against you.

But this door has been opened and through those gates came gushing wonder, magic and self-awareness and when I get to take a breather, I realize I've gained so much. And through that gain, I've learned to like myself ... just a bit, or as much as the universe will allow.

But the clarity of that open door also allows me peer into the depths of it all. Good and bad. The bad has a way of sneaking through every now and then and I do and say and feel things I would never have allowed years ago. You know, before that whole "deep end" theory came about. Sometimes my behavior scares me because I never thought I was capable of blatantly disregarding hearts. It's terrible when I know when I'm doing it. What's even worse is being hyper-aware of it. Telling myself what I'm doing is wrong. What I'm saying is wrong. How I'm not holding hearts up as high as I once promised with these very same fingers. Sometimes I am a monster. One that steps on flowers, curses the heavens and thinks about pushing old women into traffic. I wish I could turn it off. I wish I could plug up the holes and just allow for sunlight. I'm trying so goddamn hard to be a better person but my methods are clumsy. Like aiming at apples on heads using hand grenades. Gets the job done, but someone loses an arm in the process.

I have awakened the monster and I can't get him to go back or to be what he once was. Sleeping and quiet. When he wasn't a threat. When I wasn't capable of the things I now do. When I thought twice. When I wasn't afraid of the future ... because I want it to go away. To sew it back up. To send it packing. So that I can truly grow and believe in myself the way the kids do. But I thank god they can't see what I truly am.

Promise Keepers Anonymous
❖

I hate when motherfuckers think it's ok to bust my balls for not being able to speak Spanish.

"Where are your grandparents from?"

"Um, the West Side of Chicago."

The Mexican side of my family has been here for four generations. I wouldn't be so arrogant to walk up to you and say, "Oh, you're Italian/German/French, why don't you speak it?" I'm not that big of an arrogant prick to assume you are less than intelligent because you don't know what language your mother's father's father spoke.

I hate when people get away with acting like a spoiled, ignorant little fucks under the guise of, "But I was drunk."

Like I've always maintained, no one is ever a better person when they're stumbling around, looking for a place to vomit. Alcohol doesn't make you a bad person; it only accentuates the bad person you are inside. I've seen so many so-called respectable adults turn into racist, homophobic, pretentious and vile humans when the bars let out at 2 a.m. in my neighborhood. Men in $1000 suits calling cab drivers "sand-niggers" and pulling down street signs. Call me an elitist straight edge asshole all you like, if those fuckers weren't drunk, shit wouldn't be happening.

I hate when men think its ok to grab women's asses in bars, as if the "boys will be drunken boys" mentality excludes them from treating women with the same respect they would have in church or at a bus stop. As if the hallowed walls of a bar

141

or the flat screen TVs projecting sports somehow shield them from the outside world. Where they can drink to "have fun" by generalizing races and genders and calling women "sluts" from the safety of barstools because women won't give them the attention they so desperately crave. So in retaliation, they grope. It's not so much the sexual assault that offends me, but the arrogance that fuels the action. That they think they are somehow immune from reprisal. Truth is, they are. If someone sexually assaulted your mom while she was out looking to buy a new car, that man would be arrested. But if it's in a bar full of drunken men, well then, "Honey, you shouldn't have been wearing that short skirt." If I had one wish, it wouldn't be to erase all the sexual assaults in the world, it would be freedom from persecution for when I walk into bars, just waiting for that arrogant fuck who thinks his fun little ass-grabbing-antics won't offend or hurt women. I'd stab each and every last one of them with a dull and rusty bowie knife.

I hate the fact that I hate so much.
That I let the actions of others make me grit my teeth.

I hate that people seem to bond better when they're both complaining.
That there are corporate bonding strategies that pull teams together by having a common enemy. It's so ingrained in our social structure that it is a technique used by businesses to make more productive employees.

I hate that misery loves company.

But I love when I realize that hating and complaining sucks good life out of me. Like the saying goes, I have to be the change I want to see in the world.

You ever see those people walking around smiling? Those happy fuckers that seem to be happy just to be breathing?

They breathe the same air you do, walk the same earth, live in the same country, see and smell the same things you do. They were born with 10 toes, 10 fingers and a brain with the ability to reason and a body, heart and head that feel pain. Just. Like. You.

So why are these fuckers so goddamn happy? What do they know that you don't?

It's simple.

They realized that the sun rises and sets every day and is their ally.

A promise-keeper.

An opportunity holder.

To start again. To be better.

To finally leave behind the person they hate and be the person they deserve to be.

They realize that it's rare that anyone will ever truly believe in them, and if you sit around waiting for motherfuckers to open your door, to hand you money, to wake you up, to start your car on cold mornings, to make your job fun, to make the sun shine on sad days or find you the perfect boy ... that you'll be dead from a broken heart and old age.

It's time to kick open the doors and talk our way past security guards because I certainly don't have the patience it takes to wait around for motherfuckers to make my life easier or get right with the world. And all of those people waiting for the world to "shape up" while taking pit stops to point fingers at all the "evil-doers" of the world just make it easier for me to pass them by.

She Said

"But I don't want to try anymore, it hurts."

I took a long breath because I knew what was coming. She
didn't.
I asked her if she laughed today.
She said, "Yes."
I asked her if she has a family that loves her.
She said, "Yes."
I asked her if she still had the ability to make money,
to make friends,
to run and smile.
She said, "Yes, now what the fuck are you getting at?"

I asked if she has ever been betrayed,
Stabbed in the back,
Taken for granted,
Abused.
She said, "Yes."

I told her that the problem was her.
That she didn't even realize that she came complete with the
armor she so desperately craved. The answers she desired. The
coping mechanisms she cried out for.
They were all right in front of her. No, they were in her. On
her.
They were the magic that kept her feet in motion.

145

I told her that she's been walking through fire all along and never once stopped to look in the mirror and appreciate the glorious woman she had been forged into. That she had been to hell, got kicked in the vagina and came back loving. I told her that I learned a valuable lesson years ago the hard way. That if you weren't dead, you could still put one foot in front of the other and that each step forward was a step further away from the hurt.

I told her that not trying was suicide.
But breathing in and out, putting one foot in front of the other, smiling, not stopping ... well, that was loving.

That was learning to love yourself.

Wednesday, February 20, 2008
4:01 a.m. Chicago, IL
❖

They ask me what keeps me moving and I make jokes about being too stupid to quit. That the race has been finished and I refuse to stop running after the rabbit.

Truth is, I need hope.

Like the Christians and the scientologists and democrats and junkies of the world. We need hope, and I don't know how to do much, at least no more than your average. Tenacity is what sets people apart. But I've found there are two types of successful people. The first is those who didn't give up because they wouldn't let themselves: the marathon runners, doctors and mountain climbers. The ones who had a singular goal, whose focus and conviction were unwavering. Like Dr. King, who stood in the face of rocks and insults, and he marched forward in defiance for the rights of the individual. Equality was the finish line and he gave up his life striving toward it.

The other types are the ones with no other choice: your fighters, writers and Tupacs of the world. The people who *do* because they don't know how *not* to. The people who fight because they have no other choice. Because they possess the power to smash things with their fists, and that's all they've ever been good at. Those who can't walk a straight line or manage a high school relationship but can entertain thousands of people from a stage for an hour a night and send women into fits of orgasm and men into raging bouts of envy.

We are the people who chase the rabbit.

We run because, outside of that track, the world seems hopelessly average and we know that hope never sprung from

151

mediocrity.

    We run because there is hope in the journey.

    We don't run for the goal, we run because it's all we know.

Monday, February 25, 2008
2:51 p.m. Chicago, IL

❖

    Lying in my bedroom, looking at the boxes that are piled to the ceiling, I can't help but wonder what will become of this. Not only the thousands of books, DVDs, CDs and the like, but what will become of this? The Deadxstop Publishing Company. It was a necessity, born out of "nowhere else to turn" and a naive do-it-yourself spirit. It all sounds good while spoken in feverish rants in the back of coffeehouses but really, on paper, no one in their right mind would enter into this world and realistically expect to see a speck of success. Granted, success is subjective, but a certain amount of monetary success must follow or that idealistic success gets steamrolled by expensive spoiled children, health insurance payments, overdue cable bills and other "real world" responsibilities. But where will I end up?

    Will I be a footnote to a story told over dinner?

    A long forgotten guide to someone's childhood?

    Or a punch line to a joke made by an anonymous commentor on a message board?

    Do I possess the energy to keep up the fight? To continuously rage against intolerance and stand in the face of life-wasters and time-fuckers?

    Even if I do, will anyone still listen?

    Will they out-grow me like Christopher Robin to his Pooh?

Will my fury be dulled down to a prosaic roar? Huh?
Will I know when to quit?
Is quitting an option?
Do I even want to entertain it as an option?

I've accepted my fate. This is my life. This way of living,
seeing and consuming. I'm more than ok with this. But will the
community continue to embrace me and be my collective little
angel that makes this dream a reality? I would be lying if I told
you I didn't think about it. Often. But this is all I know. I've tried
the other ways and how they weigh my feet to the pavement on
those walks home from the train. I know the shoulder sloping
defeat they stab you with, day after day. I know the dread of
tomorrow.

But now, at this second, I know what the promise of
tomorrow beams. I know I get to see countries I've never seen
and meet people I only know from e-mails and comments. I
know at 33 years old, that the best days are still ahead of me
and that after you've kicked down a few doors, it just becomes
second nature.

I don't want this to end.

I see how people pour every last drop of their lives into
dreams that look more than ridiculous to the outside world and
how they crash back to earth after a handful of years. How they
melt back into the crowd and seethe in anger at having to pay
for concerts, clothes and dinners. How they fizzle out. How they
reluctantly fade away into what they had always done battle with.
That mindset. That world.

I am terrified of losing my gleam.

I promise you this. I will fight. I will stand eye-to-eye
with those dark clouds looking to envelope my dream, pound

my chest with all that I have left in me, die to make this real. For you, for me, and for every last person with a "ridiculous" dream. I promise.

An Albatross Revisited
❖

You know, I never intended to write about it, much less talk about it. It is the most haunting memory I have. One that was burned so deeply across my eyes that I hid it from myself for years.

After my speakings, I usually have a question and answer period where I say, "You can ask me anything your little heart desires." Don't worry about offending me or asking anything too personal. I've been asked everything from my penis size to how much money I make to what is the best way to kill a puppy. See, I want the audience to truly understand that I have nothing to hide. By this example, I'm attempting to demonstrate that there is freedom in vulnerability. That there, standing behind nothing but a microphone is a kid with flaws, inconsistencies and hypocrisies and is still willing to be scrutinized by a group of strangers.

A woman recently asked the question, "Do you feel that by putting yourself out there to be consumed you won't have anything left for yourself?"

I took a drink to give it some thought, then I responded.

"I don't want anything for myself. The way I see it is, the more I put out, the less the horrors weigh on my back."

And this is truth for me. I know that I come off as some self-important guy with a martyr complex, but in all reality, it's a selfish act. Fuck, I don't want these things. That's why we keep them packaged up in the deepest oceans of our heads and hearts, because they fucking suck. They hurt and destroy friendships, relationships and everyday life. They prevent us from ever truly connecting out of fear. Apprehension and reluctance are direct

157

results of how your uncle or babysitter touched you wrong. The animosity we feel for our fathers fosters a fear of abandonment. The hostility we feel toward our mothers who told us we were "fat" or "ugly" manifests itself later in life as resentment towards other women and is the basis for our self-loathing. That we never got our grandfathers to hold our hands, or to lie next to our fathers, or to be held by our mothers. That our opportunities to connect with our loved ones the way we so desperately needed have been stolen, ruined or lost to the years.

That is what I attempt to "talk" away. Those are the black spots I speak of, and I want to leave them somewhere in a basement cafe in Birmingham, in Montréal, in Houston, in Brooklyn…

I go on to explain that I was never a writer. I never did exceptionally well in school. I dropped out of community college, and I never felt the compulsion to read all that much. I only wrote because when I bashed the keys, it was my equivalent to punching a heavy bag or screaming into a pillow. Regardless of quality, context or capability, I've always felt a certain level of relief afterward. I explain that I never could have imagined the strength and accountability I have taken from exposing my secrets. Because anyone who ever called themselves an artist has an obligation to pull out their guts, slap them inside a book, on a canvas, into a microphone to create true art and give back with the same loyalty the audience gives them. And I owe them that much.

If you can sit in a seat for 90 minutes and listen to me, buy my wears and hug me before you leave, well I owe you that much of your life back. I owe you 90 minutes of faith, and the only way I know how to do that is to pull from every last corner, every last hurtful place and say, "Here it is and this is why I think it is," to the best of my ability.

I told her that my theory was that there is strength in vulnerability. I told her about the first story I ever wrote that I felt a sense of ease when I left it behind. When I put it out to consume. It was the story about my little brother, Eric, who was killed when he was young. It was one paragraph. Simple. It was called, "an albatross."

The worst memory I have is from 1983.
I got a baby brother a few years earlier. He was almost 3. I was in 3rd grade.
It's still fuzzy. What I do remember was it was summer, warm and the sun was mid-way down in one of those blood red and orange sunsets that postcards were made for. My next-door neighbor Roy and I were going run up to the bowling alley to play video games.
As we were walking through my front lawn my brother Eric came running out asking if he could go with, I yelled, "NO, get back in the house." my mom asks if we can take him with... "NO, go away!" I scream and start walking faster.
He starts running after us saying all he wants to do is play. All he wants is to be with his big brother, all he wants is a companion; all he wants is to be included.
And we run. Only looking back to see him with his arms out crying at the end of the yard.
He was killed the next spring.

Reading that paragraph I wrote four years ago makes my stomach drop and leaves me with a mix of nausea and uncleanliness. It is horrible.

After the accident, the deaths, the funerals, the flowers, the crying, the splitting of my family and the make-up tests at school ... it was all I was left with. That memory. That fucking memory that I could not shake. I would lie in my grandfather's bed at night and punch the sides of my head. I would hit in hopes that I could shake or damage something enough that it would cause me to forget. And I would cry myself into heaving fits, ones that would cause me to froth at the corners of my mouth and clench my little brown hands into fists. I would get up and walk to the dark bathroom where I would lie down on the cold tile floor and curl up in a ball. It was the only way I knew how to get back to sleep. I didn't deserve to be in a warm bed. Not after what I did. Not after I ran away from my brother. A child. Who I would never again get to see. For years I would do this. Lie on the tile of a cold and dark bathroom and violently bash the sides of my head.

Over the course of a couple of years, those nights slowly faded and tapered off, so much so that the day my mother casually brought up in conversation how odd it was that I would sleep on the bathroom floor when I was younger, that feeling of nausea instantly rushed back. That albatross. It rushed across my eyes as an adult and, all at once, I saw Eric's face and arms stretched out, the colors of the sky, the length of the grass and the angles of my house. It was more than I could take as an adult. But that memory was what set into motion this great purge. This theory that by neatly placing each one of the nights, the abuse, the deaths on a table on a screen in a book that you, yes you, could help it all just make a little sense in my head. That the kids, the audience, my saviors could stop that little boy from smashing the memories from his temples.

My theory held up.

Four years after writing that paragraph, I have invested my heart, my money and all I have into that theory.

I can never bring back dead brothers, and I can't push away the sexual abuse, the scars of cutting or the abandonment of family. But I can accept it, roll around in it for a while, remember the sights and smells; paint it, write it and display it. I can't change it. It will never go away. I can never make those days different. But I can dig and dissect to see how they played a role into who I am today and hopefully prevent them from stealing any more of the spark in my eyes and the magic in my fingers. So when you see me, standing there on that stage, that is the visualization of my theory put to test. That is me selfishly throwing the reckless garbage from my life at you ... in hopes that you see the great it has done for these eyes. That still fight for magic.

Joseph

❖

I initially thought it would be a better way to meet girls. You know, doing hair and all. I figured all I needed was to become a male hair stylist and things would all come together. I saw the way women fawned over them. They took their word as gospel. All women love to be told they're pretty and beautiful. While strange men handing out compliments has an air of motive, when you're a man whose sole job description is to make women look younger and prettier, your compliments become legitimate.

So I went to school and got my cosmetology license. Then I got a job at a nice salon on the Magnificent Mile in Chicago. Then I assisted and put in my time in the trenches shampooing and sweeping up hair. Eventually, I ended up with my own chair, what I worked years to attain.

Did I meet women? Yes.

I became everything I thought I would. I smiled and told women that I could make them appear hip, fresh and more vibrant. (How can a hair color make you look thinner? Plus, you already said this two grafs up.) And they believed me ... because I did. I learned fast and built up clientele even faster. I always hugged my clients and left them with an, "It was nice hanging out with you today." I learned to always leave clients with a compliment. I liked leaving them with a positive last impression, I thought it would lure them back. It did.

What I never thought much about were the people I would meet from so many different walks of life. Women who wouldn't spit on me if I were on fire were now telling me their darkest secrets. Women who were cheating on their husbands. Women who were stealing their husband's money. Women who ran houses of prostitution. Women who were prostitutes. Women who openly admitted they married for money. They came in day after day to tell me about their children, their careers, their secrets, their affairs, their money, their aspirations, their hopes and their prayers. And I ate it up.

I also took no offense when they inevitably mouthed the words, "I can tell you because you will never meet anyone I know."

I was their secret-keeper. Their confidant.

I had an almost exclusively female clientele. Maybe three or four male clients who came in for their bi-monthly, all-over color, gray hair touch up. That's why I found it a bit odd when I was booked to do a full head of highlights on a male. It was a Sunday and only a fraction of the stylists were working. Notoriously a slow day, it was more about reading and putting in hours than sitting with fingers crossed, hoping for a walk-in customer. But that Sunday, that's what I got.

I stepped into our reception hall where a well-dressed man in his early 40s sat in our plush chairs while sipping on cranberry juice.

"Joseph?" I asked.

He stood and the first thing I noticed was his smile. It was instant and genuine.

Working where I worked and presenting a new client with my adorned facade made for an interesting and usually very awkward first few minutes. I was well aware of what they were thinking, because they usually confessed to me later in the year after we had built up enough of a report.

"No offense, but I thought you were going to give me a pink mohawk," they would say with a mouth covered giggle.

I am not a stupid kid. I understand that the spectacle I've made of myself turns off a certain segment of the civilian population. I'm fine with that. But as a person whose job it is to apply chemicals to hair and make people look not only presentable but spectacular, well, it makes gaining the confidence of a introductory client that much more difficult.

"Hello, Joseph. My name is Christopher, follow me to my station."

He sat down in my chair, lurched forward to get a closer look in the mirror and began fluffing his chin length hair.

"Our computers have you down for a full highlight, is this correct?" I asked.

"Yes. I need to look younger and more hip. I'm going to be hosting a television show."

Interesting, I thought. But I made a point to never ask a client what they did for a living when they first sat down. I like to get to know a person first before I inevitably judge them on their profession. It was a little game I liked to play. I would ask my usual handful of questions and would try and guess what they did for money in my head.

After a short consultation, I walked back to the dispensary and began mixing up the hair color. I returned and began setting up my foils and hair clips. It was eating at me and who was I to pretend that I wasn't mildly impressed by him hosting a television show. So, I bit.

"So, tell me about this show you're hosting."

He went on to tell me that it was a money marketing show and that he was being brought in as an expert. I thought, shit, poor people don't get brought in as "experts" on the matters of money, he must be doing something right and since I always saw everybody that sat in my chair as a resource, I probed even further.

"So, why did they choose you as their expert?"

He told me it was because he owned a mortgage refinancing company with multiple locations and had made a bit of a name for himself. I was impressed, and he seemed to like to talk about himself as most people do, so I sat back, let him do all the talking and took mental notes. He grew up in the town next to mine and he came from the very low end of the middle class. When he was in high school, he said he always wanted money so he wouldn't have to live like his parents.

Now, I've heard that sentence before. It usually prefaces a very lengthy capitalistic selfish rant that attempts to justify selling out values and stepping over little people to get where they, "need to be." But what Joseph was saying didn't come off as arrogant, self-righteous or crass. He said he wanted to give his parents the lives they deserved and to give his children the educations he could never afford. Sure, I've heard the same thing come out of adults' mouths before, usually to excuse their employment at some multi-national, ethic-less corporation, but something in his voice led me to believe that he might just be a genuine exception.

There was something in his tone and swag that reeled me in. He had all of the flash and personality of a rock star combined with a magician yet lacked the creepy used car-salesman tactics. He spoke and I listened. I took furious mental notes, and when his eyes lit up, I paid special attention. He spoke about what accomplishments and attaining goals did for his spirit. I was jealous of his devotion. I wanted to be inside his skin, to be so absolute in a destination. To believe in something so strongly that it ceased being a job and evolved into a love affair. He said that he looked forward to the office every morning. That his wealth was in his children playing on beaches and the ability to provide his mother with stability and comfort.

It was over before I knew it. His hair was done processing and I had to relinquish him to the shampoo girls. I walked with him to the shampoo room. Here I was, me, walking next to this man worth millions, a man who had made a life for him from a simple idea, an obsession and a refusal to stay down; and now here he was, telling me his secrets.

He sat down, leaned his head back in the bowl and the shampoo girl began rinsing his hair.

"Joseph, it was amazing talking with you. Take care of yourself."

I was turning into a fan, I couldn't help it. Embarrassed, I turned to walk away when he said, "Christopher?"

"Yeah?"

"Look, I know you have a job here but if you ever think about changing careers, give me a call. I promise you will make no less than six figures your first year."

He pulled a card from his pocket and handed it to me. It read, "President."

The entire train ride home that night, I stood and stared at that card. What it meant. I walked through the door of my basement apartment and told the story to my friends. They asked what I was going to do, all I could respond with was, "I don't know."

I waited a few days before I called. The receptionist mentioned that she knew who I was and was expecting my call. Odd. She asked if I would be interested in coming down to take a look at the office, I said sure, so we set a date.

A few days later, I managed to get a ride out to the suburbs and was dropped off in front of a large and very tall building. I was dressed as nice as I could, there may or may not have been a tie involved. I stepped out of the elevator and walked up to a woman sitting behind a desk answering phones.

"Excuse me, my name is Christopher Gutierrez, I have an appointment?"

She directed me to a row of chairs and said that someone would be with me in a minute. A few minutes passed and a woman approached, I stood, we shook hands and I gathered all of my manners and went into instant customer service mode. She walked me down a hall and I saw offices and cubicles, men in suits and women in sensible heels. I feel that at any minute someone was going to recognize me and whisper, "Isn't that the guy who ate a banana cream pie out of that one boys ass for money?"

She showed me the conference room, the presentation room and the lunchroom. After we made our rounds, we sat down in her office where she told me how much money she made last year. More than I have made in my entire life, combined. She continued to talk about the benefits of the job and how lucrative it was. I stopped her mid-sentence and said, "I'm sorry to interrupt, but I was under the impression that this was an interview."

She looked puzzled and waited a breath or two to respond.

"Joseph already interviewed you. At the salon."

She continued to talk about the benefits of the job but I couldn't seem to pay attention. I kept thinking, he interviewed me? I imagined I came off more like an over-achieving, bush-league interviewer that forgot to take his Ritalin that day. Joseph obviously saw something in me that he liked, so much so that he not only gave me his card but hired me on the spot. The woman wasn't interviewing me, she was showing me around my new office. I had been instructed to call and set up an appointment to begin my training. That thought left me in a daze until I got home that day.

I sat on my couch that night and went back and forth. I would be required to work six days a week, 10-hour days. I would have to buy suits, many suits and possibly a briefcase. I would have clients and people who were depending on me with the biggest investment of their lives. I was aware of the responsibilities, and I won't lie, I was a bit intimidated. But that was the aspect that actually pushed me towards the job. I liked the challenge.

I picked up the phone, held the card out in front of me and thought about the sacrifices I would be expected to make. No more night-time bike rides through downtown Chicago. No more touring with bands. No book tours and any thoughts of taking my writing seriously would be put on an indefinite hold. Immediately, I thought of my client who came in every few months to get her highlights touched up and listen to me talk at her for two hours. The one thing I never expected from my clients was the fact that they loved to hear my stories. Just as their lives were foreign and intriguing to me, mine was to them as well. My client would tell me how she went to school for creative writing and always wanted to write a book. She was envious of my life. Mine. Simply because I had had just finished my manuscript. I told her that my life wasn't as cool as she thought it was and that I lived paycheck to paycheck. She said that the only necessities in the world were food, love and passion.

She told me about the regret she had because she never pursued her one passion, writing. I told her everyone has a story to write, and that it would be an amazing gift to leave for her daughter or grandkids. She sighed and looked at the ground. She was an attorney.

That client, and many others, showed me how unimportant money is compared to the gold of chasing a dream.

I set my phone down and made a decision right then and there. I said aloud, "Ok Chris, don't take the job. But if you're not, you do this shit for real." I wanted to take a shot, a real fucking shot at something. I wanted to know that feeling, that intensity that Joseph had in his words when he sat in my chair at the salon that Sunday. I knew that working for that company would beat my soul. And I wasn't ready to give up my childish dreams just yet. No one ever aspires to become assistant managers at video stores or pizza delivery guys, I've been both, I speak from experience. The people who end up in those positions are forced there because of circumstances beyond their control or because they gave up.

Maybe I'm a fool. I'm sure there are plenty of people who would kill to have been given an opportunity to work for a company like Joseph's. But I'm sure there are just as many people out there with four car garages, jacuzzis and health insurance willing to give it all up for one more shot. One more run against the wind for an idea they believe in.

That night, I stepped outside at two in the morning, got on my bike and pedaled down Oakdale Avenue towards Lake Michigan.

I said it. I made sure to say it out loud. To make it real.

"Do this shit for real."

I said it again as I felt the cold wind across my cheeks and I swerved through the traffic of taxis and late night drunks.

That year I published my first book.

A couple years later, I quit working for someone else, packed up my books and began driving town to town, for an idea.

Because I have to do this shit for real.

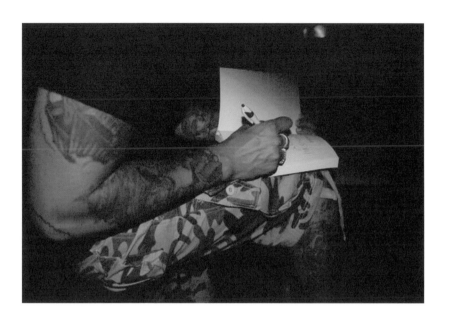

About the Author:

Christopher Gutierrez is a freelance writer living and loving in
Chicago.
This is his third book.

Also by Christopher Gutierrez:

On the Upswing of Life, Love and Regret

A Life Deliberate

The Dirt of an Electric Boy (Spoken Word CD)

Make Your Mark (DVD)

Thank you friends.